THE LOCAL

From Chris & Pam
& Pierce
My Birthday
2003.

THE LOCAL
ALES & TALES *of the* WEST COUNTRY

by

Chris Denham

DENHAM BOOKS

First published in Great Britain by Denham Books Ltd. 1999

British Library Cataloguing in Publication Data
A Catalogue Record for this book is available from the British Library.

ISBN 0 9536905 0 4

DENHAM BOOKS
Walkespool
Kingston
Kingsbridge
Devon
TQ7 4PY

Tel: 01548 810231

Design and illustrations by Jennifer Johnson
Photographs: Julia Hobson, Joe Murphy & Victoria Dawe

Printed by Kingfisher Print & Design, Totnes, Devon TQ9 5XN
Bound by Folio Bookbinders, Brislington, Bristol

CONTENTS

DARTMOOR & SURROUNDS

Pages 74-105

SOUTH DEVON

Pages 106-145

EAST CORNWALL

WEST CORNWALL & THE ISLES OF SCILLY

ACKNOWLEDGEMENTS

Anyone who has pursued the life-long passion of Pub Hunting will recognise the need for a tolerant family, so thanks are due first of all to my wife, Sally, and to my children, Andrew and Tessa, who have allowed me to indulge my hobby. Thanks also go to Sally for editing this book, and for doing all the boring administrative bits.

I'm grateful to Joe Murphy, Julia Hobson and Victoria Dawe for taking the photographs - I hope I have introduced them to some good pubs along the way! In addition, I must thank Frank Gibson and Steve Watt for their photographic contributions from the Isles of Scilly. My good friend Jennifer Johnson has done the illustrations and design work, and I am indebted to her.

As an avid reader of anything to do with pubs, I must also pay due respects to authors like Michael Jackson for his many wonderful books on the subject; to Andrew Barr for his fascinating book "Drink, A Social History"; and to countless historians, professional and amateur, who have passed on stories of pubs, West Country villages, and ale through the ages.

Thanks to Westcountry Television for giving me the opportunity to make television programmes about my favourite subject, and to the many viewers who seem to have enjoyed "The Local". It could not have been done without directors Howard Perks and Matt Bennett. Cheers. We filmed most of our "Tales from the Snug" by the fireside of one of my favourite pubs, The Miner's Arms in Hemerdon, where David and Linda Honey have always been examples of the perfect licensees. I promise to replace the logs!

The tour around pubs in the Westcountry would not have been nearly as much fun without my faithful old car, Doris, so thanks to Haydon Rider at Haytor Sports and Vintage for first introducing me to the old girl, and to George Richardson and Tom Hendy for their mechanical expertise which has kept her on the road.

It is arguable that there would be no proper pubs to write about without the sterling efforts of the Campaign for Real Ale, which has done so much to preserve them. Thanks to all CAMRA members, and long may you continue the good work. Last, but by no means least, special thanks must go to all the landlords, landladies, barmaids, barmen and 'regulars' who have made the production of the television programmes, and the writing of this book, such an enjoyable experience.

INTRODUCTION

There is no institution in the world to rival the British pub. While other nations with a century or two of history to their names may have their share of palaces, castles and stately homes, none of them can lay claim to anything which comes close to that special place tucked down the back street of a town, or in the village square, or nestling in remote countryside, where for a thousand years or more the British have gathered to enjoy good company, good ale and good fun.

I have always loved pubs and been a passionate pub hunter, so when, in 1998, I was asked to make a series of programmes for Westcountry Television about the region's great watering holes, it did not take a great deal to persuade me, especially when they accepted my suggestion that I should travel around in a lovely old motor car, a 1936 Rover 12 Tourer. I affectionately named her Doris, after a favourite barmaid who, like the car, was built for comfort rather than speed.

Making the series was like re-creating a journey I had undertaken thirty years ago in another old open-top car, when I was first introduced to the delights of West Country pubs. Much has changed in the intervening years, and many old favourites have been transformed into glorified restaurants which just happen to serve beer, or have been tarted up in such a way as to destroy all the original character, but many others have survived, apparently oblivious to the passing of the years. In this book I have described some of my personal favourite pubs in the region. I must confess to a bias in favour of plain, 'unspoilt' pubs, but I hope I have included a wide enough range to appeal to all tastes. I have enjoyed drinking in all of them.

The only word of warning I ought to give is that many pubs do seem to change hands with monotonous regularity. A pub is only as good as the person behind the bar, and while I have tried to keep my information as up-to-date as possible, things may have changed since the time of writing.

However, even new landlords can't change the stories behind the pubs themselves, and as readers will discover, many pubs are living records of English history. This fact was even given 'official' recognition back in 1872 by politician Sir William Harcourt when he declared, "As much of the history of England has been brought about in public houses as in the House of Commons".

The real English pub is an endangered species. Changing drinking habits, cheap foreign booze, high taxes and the problems of just getting to and from the pub, are forcing many of them out of business. However, they can still be found and I, for one, think it is important to support them and enjoy them before it is too late.

I hope that this book will go some way to encouraging more people to support their local, and to securing the future success of that great British institution, The Pub.

Chris Denham – September 1999

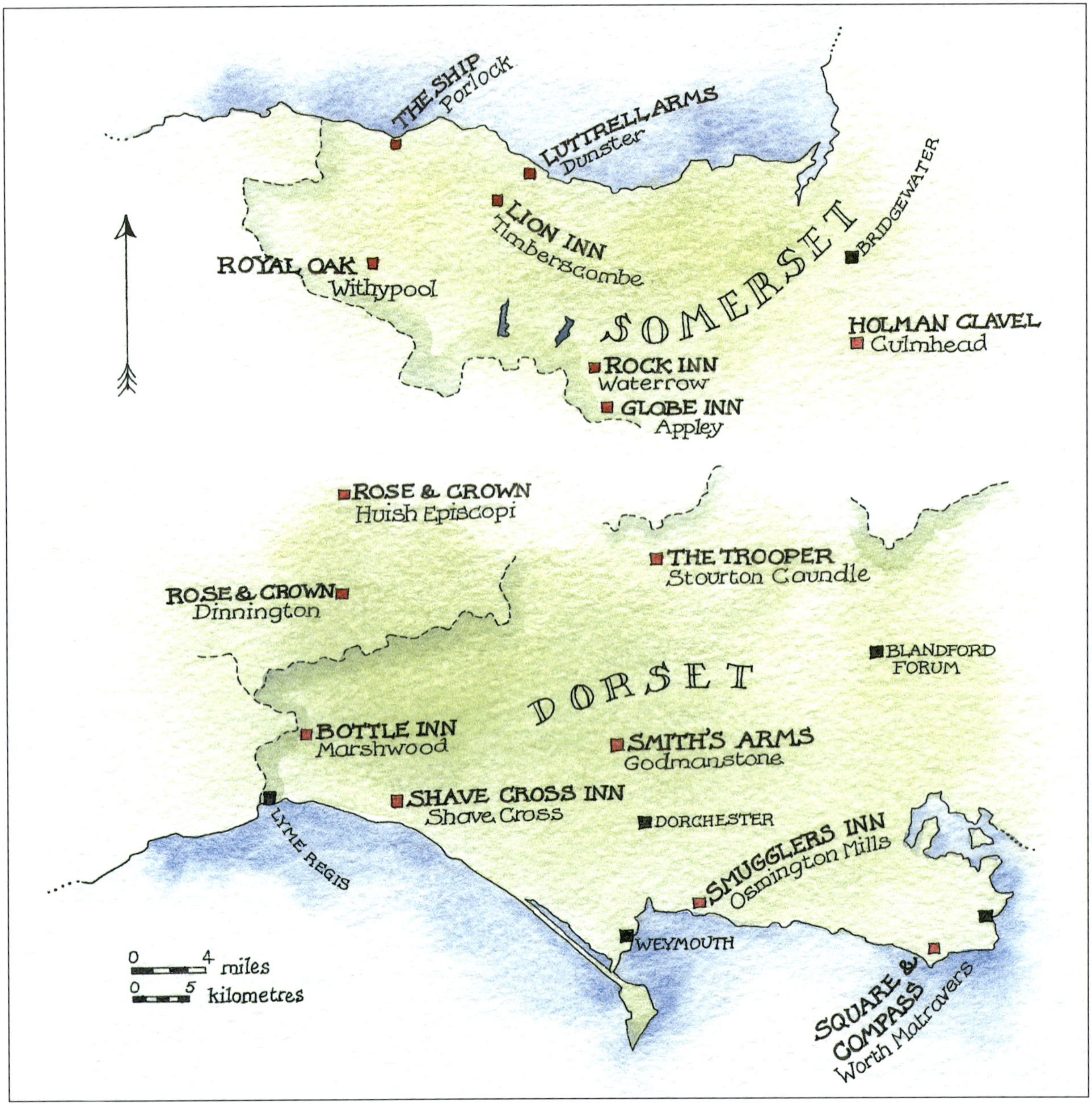
THE SHIP
Porlock
LUTTRELL ARMS
Dunster
LION INN
Timberscombe
ROYAL OAK
Withypool
SOMERSET
BRIDGEWATER
HOLMAN CLAVEL
Culmhead
ROCK INN
Waterrow
GLOBE INN
Appley
ROSE & CROWN
Huish Episcopi
THE TROOPER
Stourton Caundle
ROSE & CROWN
Dinnington
BLANDFORD
FORUM
DORSET
BOTTLE INN
Marshwood
SMITH'S ARMS
Godmanstone
SHAVE CROSS INN
Shave Cross
DORCHESTER
LYME REGIS
SMUGGLERS INN
Osmington Mills
WEYMOUTH
SQUARE & COMPASS
Worth Matravers
0 4 miles
0 5 kilometres

Dorset & Somerset

BOTTLE INN

Marshwood

On the B3165 between Crewkerne and Axminster.

Before modern brewing methods developed in the last couple of centuries, all beer could fairly have been described as "organic" with no nasty chemicals, nitrates or artificial preservatives. Now there's a strong move to return to such natural products, and the Bottle Inn at Marshwood is leading the way.

The food menu makes use of organic meats and vegetables, the wine list features organically produced wines, and there is a wide selection of bottled organic lagers and ciders. The pub is also one of the first in the country to sell an organic draught beer, Caledonian, produced in Scotland. Its motto is "save the planet with a pint", but I am going to have to put my worthy ambitions on hold as I found Caledonian something of an acquired taste. For Philistines like me, there is a good draught Otter on sale.

The Bottle is in a 500 year old building, and was first mentioned as an ale house back in the 1600s. It got its name after becoming the first pub in the area to sell bottled beer, as opposed to the stuff served in a jug. The two small bars have remained substantially unchanged over the years, and there still remains a remarkable old meat smoker above the large open fireplace. Chunks of meat and fish would be placed in this wooden cage on the ceiling, and left there in the smoke from the fire which was directed through the contraption, until it was cooked. At least that is the theory. In practice it must have showered the drinkers below with dripping hot grease, but perhaps the strong ale made them oblivious.

In recent years the Bottle Inn has become famous for its connection with nettles. One day back in 1987 two locals were having an argument in the bar about the size of the nettles on their land, each claiming to have the tallest. The landlady decided to settle things by arranging a contest which captured the imagination of the locals, there not being a lot of other live entertainment at the time. The Marshwood Annual Longest Nettle Competition was born. Everywhere else in the country gardeners curse the things, but here they are almost worshipped. On an evening in July the locals bring their prize specimens to the Bottle for formal judging amid much barracking and jollification. A crate of ale is the prize, and a bob or two is also raised for local charities.

When one chap brought in a fifteen footer he foolishly announced that if anyone beat it, he would eat the nettle. Naturally another local found a twenty footer and so another competition was born. On a weekend around Mid-summer Day the people of Marshwood can be seen chomping their way through yard upon yard of stinging weeds for the annual Nettle Eating Competition.

Who said we English don't know how to make our own entertainment? What's more, its organic.

Real Ales: Caledonian, Otter, Wadworths 6X.

GLOBE INN

Appley

As the crow flies, this is 6 miles west of Wellington. If you haven't got a crow with you, try a map and enjoy the lanes!

The pub hunter's quest takes him/her to some stunning parts of the countryside, well away from the usual well-trodden tourist routes. Despite all the problems of survival facing country pubs, it is gratifying to know that interesting, well-run watering holes can still be found buried deep in rural areas.

To the west of Wellington in Somerset lies just such an area, gently rolling hills, leafy lanes and delightful villages. Considering there are so few chimney pots around, it has a remarkable number of good pubs, and one which is definitely worth seeking out is the Globe at Appley. It is not the easiest pub to find. Signposts are few and far between, but it is worth the effort.

Appley is one of five hamlets which are collectively known as Staulley Parish. Not so long ago agriculture was the main source of employment for the men of the area and the Globe Inn was a typical farmhouse/ale house where the farm workers would come to be served cider and beer straight from the barrel, to be quaffed in the 'kitchen'. In spite of most of the farm workers having been replaced by machines, not much has changed. The customers at the Globe are different, but the pub itself appears to have hardly altered.

The bar is little more than a serving hatch alongside the main corridor, and off that corridor there are three small rooms full of comfortable cottage tables and chairs for eaters and drinkers. They look and feel like homely sitting rooms in a private house. The emphasis in the pub today is very much on the food, good home cooking with original dishes on the menu, and there is a more formal dining room at the rear of the pub which is used in the evenings.

The colour scheme in the pub is striking! Reds, pinks, purples and blues. It may sound over the top, but somehow it seems just right for the place.

Real Ales: Cotleigh.

TALES FROM THE SNUG

The rest of the world is increasingly appreciating the delights of British beer, and every day around one and a half million pints of it is being drunk abroad. The USA is our biggest customer, and you can now get a pint of British beer in around a hundred countries. The one thing you can't get, despite all the best efforts of foreign nations, is the unique atmosphere of the English pub.

HOLMAN CLAVEL

Culmhead

From Blagdon Hill head north towards Taunton.

The name sounds more like a builders' merchants than a pub, and you probably won't find Culmhead on anything other than an Ordnance Survey map, but don't be put off. This is another great pub worth tracking down.

The unusual name comes from holly ('holman'), and beam ('clavel'), and refers to the lintel in the huge inglenook fireplace.

Dating back to the 14th century, the building had many different lives before becoming a pub around a hundred years ago. Originally, it was a resting place for monks as they made their pilgrimages across the country, and it is from this period that Charlie, the pub's most famous resident, survives.

Charlie is apparently the ghost of a defrocked monk. No one knows why he was defrocked, but it was probably something to do with drink, as he refuses to leave the bar. He has a habit of moving ornaments around and making objects fly off walls. Some items of tableware disappear and others get smashed. I am assured that Charlie is only being playful. Charlie became so notorious that, a few years ago, a television crew decided to spend the night in the pub to prove his existence. They were awoken in the middle of the night by the sound of a ball being hurled down the skittle alley and skittles mysteriously falling over, with no player in sight. Paranormal, or just a television crew after one drink too many? Who cares, it makes a good story.

Early in the 18th century the building was used as a school for unmarried mothers, but there is nothing recorded to show how Charlie the spectral monk reacted to their presence.

During World War II there was a small airfield at Culmhead, one of three bases in the Blackdown Hills. This one was manned by members of the Polish Airforce.

The Holman Clavel has an excellent reputation for its food and, at the same time, remains a proper, welcoming pub with the emphasis on good beers and ciders. The skittle alley extends into the dining area and, if there is an important match taking place, diners may be asked to move. They get their priorities right in this pub, which is probably why it attracts such a good crowd of friendly locals.

You will be doing a useful service to the local community by drinking here, as the pub is owned by Otterford Parish Council which gets a small slice of the price of every pint you buy, just like the Royal Oak in Meavy (described elsewhere in this little tome). It has to be a good way of paying your local taxes!

Real Ales: Butcombe and guest ales.

TALES FROM THE SNUG

When food was short, beer was very often the most important source of nutrition for the poor. It was cheaper than bread. Yet in the 17th century the authorities tried to stop so much grain being used in the brewing industry. In Somerset they closed many ale houses "in regard of the dearth of grain...and the extraordinary quantity of corn that is spent in those places".

LION INN

Timberscombe

On the A396, a few miles south of Dunster.

The main road from Tiverton to Minehead used to run straight past the door of the Lion Inn, and then they built a by-pass. Timberscombe reverted to being a quiet country village, and the pub lost all that lucrative passing trade. The pub might have died but for salvation in the form of cricket.

This whole area lives for the game. Every Sunday and Tuesday during the summer the Timberscombe Cricket Club has a game against touring sides from all over England, and occasionally from overseas. It came as a surprise to me that there were so many cricket teams on tour. They all come to this part of west Somerset to play on some of the loveliest grounds in the country, and the pitch at Timberscombe is one of the best. When the Timberscombe team is not entertaining visitors, they are involved in training and coaching sessions, so hardly a day goes by without members of the team popping into the Lion for refreshment.

Landlord Kevin Godfrey freely admits that, but for the cricketers, the pub would not survive. He also happens to be a passionate player of the game, but his position in the batting order is dictated by commitments at his pub. When he is on particularly good batting form he has been known to leave the crease 'not out' in order to dash back and open up. Frustrating, but necessary. At one stage, the pub got through four landlords in eight years, but now it looks as if Kevin may be here to stay. For a cricket loving landlord, it is a dream come true.

You don't have to be a cricket lover to appreciate the Lion Inn, but it helps. Until comparatively recently it had just a small bar, but that has now been moved and extended to accommodate more drinkers. It is the sort of large bar, unencumbered by dining tables, which encourages a jolly, lively atmosphere. For those in search of solids, there is a separate dining area.

The Lion is reputed to be one of the oldest coaching inns in Somerset, going back at least 500 years. The original walls and stables are still there, but the area where the horses were once fed and watered is now a pool room for those days and nights when the cricket season is over. Upstairs there is also a popular skittle alley. Life is never dull in Timberscombe.

Real Ales: Exmoor Gold, Butcombe and, not surprisingly, Owzat.

LUTTRELL ARMS

Dunster

An imposing building at the top end of the main street. You can't miss it.

Dunster is one of those places within the Exmoor National Park which is almost too pretty for its own good. At one end of the village is the high tower on Conygar Hill, built 200 years ago and a landmark for shipping. At the other end is the castle which dominates the village. It was originally built by the Normans, and in a thousand years of occupancy it was owned by just two families, the Mohuns and the Luttrells. It has changed a lot over the years, and the red-sandstone building you see today is just three hundred years old.

In between the castle and the tower is a wide main street lined with interesting and historic buildings, including the octagonal circular Yarn Market which dates back to the 17th century, a time when wool was big business in these parts.

Up to the reign of Queen Elizabeth, this was a busy port, but that came to an end when the river silted up. Wine must have been one of the main cargoes to arrive at Dunster, as the place was originally granted its charter shortly after the Conquest, in exchange for a tun of wine valued at forty shillings, which was a lot of plonk in those days.

Naturally, tourists make a bee-line for Dunster, and much of the town is devoted to satisfying their demands. For those seeking to stay in Dunster there are several hotels, the most impressive of which is the Luttrell Arms which, at first glance, does not appear to fit into a book about local pubs. It is rather grander than my usual choice, but the place does still retain a couple of friendly bars selling a good pint. One bar is set in the 15th century Gothic Hall with a huge fireplace, sturdy beams and antiques. The other is a less ornate 'locals' bar. Prices seem higher than the average pub price, but that is only to be expected I suppose.

It has a ghost, of course. Those of a nervous disposition are advised not to sleep in Room 25 where some form of supernatural force is said to hold unfortunate victims on the bed.

The Luttrell Arms can get very busy during the holiday season but in winter it is returned to the locals.

Real Ales: Bass.

LUTTRELL ARMS HOTEL.
Luttrell Arms
Hotel
ROOMS AVAILABLE
ALL EN-SUITE
PLEASE ASK AT
RECEPTION FOR
TONIGHTS SPECIAL
RATES

ROCK INN

Waterrow

On the B3227 between Bampton and Wiveliscombe.

At first glance it seems there is nothing in Waterrow except the Rock Inn, but this was once a busy little hamlet. It nestles in a valley on the edge of the Blackdown Hills, another one of those beautiful areas which tend to be overlooked by visitors to the West Country. For those prepared to turn off the beaten track, it is full of delights, with no shortage of attractive watering holes.

The Rock Inn is around 400 years old, dating from the time when the village was known as Skirdale, from the Old Norse 'skir' meaning clear, bright, pure, and the Saxon 'dael' meaning valley. Quarrying was one of the main sources of income here and that normally means a lot of ugly scars left on the landscape, as quarry workers are not generally known for their creative talents when it comes to clearing up before they leave a site.

In this valley they were not like that. After many years of cutting away at the hills in search of rock for building material, the place was in a bit of a mess. Rather than leave it like that, the enterprising men of the village decided to put up a building incorporating the rock-face. Even more enterprisingly, they turned it into a coaching inn, conveniently placed to relieve passing horsemen of their money in exchange for a bit of bed and board. All that was some 400 years ago when the pub was called the Travellers Rest. It changed later to The Rock when there were fewer travellers around.

The Rock Inn used to be divided into a number of small drinking rooms. A previous landlord spent some of his pools winnings in knocking down the dividing walls to make a single bar, but it is still quite small and welcoming with a separate dining area. The stable block dating from the coaching days has been converted into a pool room.

Before the changes, the pub was said to be haunted by the ghost of a young girl, of whom nothing is known, and also an ex-landlady, who sadly hanged herself on the premises. Nothing has been heard of them for years, so presumably they approve of the alterations.

The Rock is fortunate in lying within range of two good local breweries whose products are kept in excellent condition.

Real Ales: Cotleigh Tawny and Exmoor Gold.

ROSE & CROWN

Dinnington

Tucked away in the country lanes, about five miles south east of Ilminster.

For some reason which nobody quite understands, the Rose and Crown is always referred to as The Docks. It is some miles from the nearest stretch of water, but that doesn't seem to matter. The title 'The Docks' now even appears on the pub sign, below the less obvious symbol for the Rose and Crown, and in the bar there are several spoof photographs of the busy working port of Dinnington.

To add to the confusion there are more photographs which suggest that Dinnington was also an important railway station, with steam trains passing within a few feet of the front of the pub. Railway enthusiasts can often be spotted in the pub scratching their heads in bewilderment, since there doesn't appear to be any reference to the line on any of their maps. It provides good spectator sport for the locals.

From all this you will gather that things are not as they may first appear in the Rose and Crown, a pub which has more than its fair share of local 'eccentrics'. It is also the home of Somerset's answer to the Red Arrows, the Green Arrows - a formation lawn-mower team. One of the locals happens to have the country's largest collection of lawn-mowers, and they are occasionally put to good use in a display of synchronised and choreographed mowing. Well, why not?

Another regular event at the pub is the meeting of the D.T.s, which is not what you might first think, as the abbreviation actually stands for Docks Transport. One of the regulars who owns an ancient Norton motorcycle got fed up with the apparent formality of the Norton Owners Club meetings, and the D.T. meetings provide a more congenial alternative. It was suggested that anyone who owned anything with wheels which was remotely old should meet up at the pub on the first Wednesday of every month for a beer and a chat. As a result the car park is frequently filled with a wonderful assortment of ancient vehicles, ranging from bicycles to tractors and priceless Rolls Royces and Lagondas.

With all this going on (and more) life is never dull at The Docks. It is another of those fine establishments which has resisted any pressure over the centuries to be prettified, and as a result it is a welcoming, unpretentious watering hole where good beer and company is guaranteed. The pub is due to change hands shortly, for the first time in twenty years, but I am assured that there are no plans for dropping any events, or for making any serious alterations to the place. There would undoubtedly be uproar if there were.

In an age when so many pubs are becoming

standardised, The Docks remains an encouraging bastion of eccentricity.

Real Ales: Butcombe, Smiles, Old Speckled Hen, guest ales.

TALES FROM THE SNUG

Dedicated beer drinkers will always argue that beer is good for you... it's a meal in a glass... its an elixir of life... it's one of the most satisfying medicines devised by man. Non-beer drinkers tend to look at us as if we are sad old fools. But our belief is based on hundreds of years of research. Indeed as recently as the last century those who chose not to drink beer were penalised. Some total abstainers applying for life insurance had to pay an additional premium!

TALES FROM THE SNUG

Drinkers today often complain about the size of the head on their beer. In the fourteenth century it was the other end of the tankard that caused the problem. In 1364 a dodgy London ale-wife was charged with selling ale in quart pots at the bottom of which she'd put an inch and a half of pitch. Now that's what I call a short measure.

ROSE & CROWN

Huish Episcopi

On the A372, a couple of miles east of Langport.

This is one of my all-time favourites! Over the years the vast majority of pubs evolve and are altered to suit the changing demands of their customers. A very few survive however, immune to the worst excesses of the 20th century. The Rose & Crown is one of these, a pub which is apparently caught in a delightful time-warp, due to it being in the hands of the same family for well over a century. The present landlady, Eileen Pittard, is as determined as ever to keep the place just as it has always been, and her children, who are following her into the business, share her attitude. The Rose & Crown is in safe hands for years to come.

For a start it has no bar. Bars are a comparatively new introduction to pubs, and before they arrived on the scene beer and cider was brought to the drinkers by pot-boys dashing to and from the barrels in the back. At the Rose & Crown drinks are still served from a small corridor where customers and pourers mingle together. At busy times it may appear a bit chaotic, but it works.

There are four small parlour rooms, one of which is dedicated to the memory of Eileen's two uncles who were killed in the First World War. When they failed to return from the trenches in France, their portraits were hung on the wall, and the room has not changed since then. It used to be the Ladies Room. The ladies would gather here for a gossip while their other halves adjourned to the Men's Kitchen for some serious drinking, and even the occasional step dancing competition. So enthusiastic were the dancers, and so heavy were their boots, that the stone floor had to be replaced.

The one change that has been introduced at the Rose & Crown is that nowadays men and women can drink together, although I know one or two old-timers who disapprove!

Although officially known as the Rose & Crown, locals still refer to the pub as Eli's, after Eileen's father, Elijah, who ran the pub for many years and put his own indelible stamp on the place.

For centuries people made their own cider here from apples grown in their own fields next door. The apple press was driven by a horse at the back of the pub. Sadly, this is one aspect of life at Eli's which has disappeared, but there is still a good range of local ciders on offer, particularly Burrow Hill Cider, in addition to well-kept beers.

Real Ales: Bass, Teignworthy, guest ales.

TALES FROM THE SNUG

In 1787 William Wilberforce made things tough for drinkers by strictly regulating the victualling trade. It led to increase in unlicensed victuallers, and in the West Country there was good deal of illicit cider selling. In the 1820s it was said that Devon and Somerset ' are overrun with common sheds by the roadside in which cider is sold in great quantities to people of both sexes.'

ROYAL OAK

Withypool

Signposted off the B3223, halfway between Dulverton and Simonsbath.

In an age when so many villages are losing all their basic facilities, Withypool is remarkable. It is only a small community, but it still has a village shop and post office, a small garage and a good pub.

In the days when Exmoor was a Royal hunting forest, Withypool was the capital of the area. King John granted free grazing for the men of the village in return for them carrying out an annual round up of the sheep on the moor. There was, after all, nothing more distracting for a Royal hunter than a great flock of ewes straying onto the path! Today, this is still important hunting country, and the walls of the main bar in the Royal Oak are covered with hunting prints and artefacts. The bar itself is in the old stable block.

Three hundred years ago, when there were active iron mines in the area, there were two pubs in the village, and the Royal Oak is the survivor. The upstairs rooms were occupied by a hat-maker and a tailor so that the miners could have a glass or two of cider while waiting to be togged up in their new working gear.

This is also Doone country, much frequented by followers of R.D.Blackmore, all determined to track down the locations referred to in "Lorna Doone". Much of the book is said to have been written whilst Blackmore was staying in Withypool. Writing it must have been a task which interfered with his social life, since hanging on the wall in one of the bars is a letter from the author, apologising for being unable to attend a party.

Another distinguished guest at the Royal Oak was General Eisenhower, who spent a three day break from the Second World War riding on the moors.

Real Ales: Exmoor.

SHAVE CROSS INN

Shave Cross

At the southern end of the Marshwood Vale, a few miles west of Bridport.

This is one of those classic Dorset pubs, thatched roof, cob and flint. Unlike so many pubs in the county, it has not given itself over entirely to the eaters, and the Shave Cross still feels like a pub where a drinker can enjoy a pint without pressure to take on solids too.

The Shave Cross owes its origins to a mysterious female saint who was buried on top of the hill at Whitchurch Canonicorum, some two miles down the road. The history of St. Candida, who was also known as St. Wite, has been lost or forgotten over the years, but back in the 14th century pilgrims travelled from far and wide to be cured by her remains, which are entombed in a plain stone chest. Below the chest are three wide openings into which the pilgrims could put whichever limb or other bit of them needed healing. Alas, some pilgrims left it too late, (or the ale at the inn was too much for them). Their bodies were removed by way of a coffin shoot sited where the bar of the pub is today.

Today's pub was originally the last refreshment stop for the pilgrims before Whitchurch. It was here they had their heads shaved, a ritual which was apparently vitally important if the cure was going to work, and for ever more the pub became known as Shave Cross. (One of the past inn-keepers was actually named Atte Shaver, or Atte the Shaver.)

Behind the pub is a peaceful garden, a feature of which is a large mural containing hidden pictures of characters and animals, which can keep children endlessly amused while the grown-ups enjoy a drink.

Real Ales: Bass, Badger, Eldridge Pope.

TALES FROM THE SNUG

In the Middle Ages, the Church dominated the lives of the English. It controlled all the Festival dates, and it gradually also took over the brewing industry. Popular pilgrimages of the day were also controlled, and recommendations were made that pilgrims stay in church-provided hostels, and enjoy church-produced booze. Payment was at the discretion of the traveller with no fixed charge, so if you didn't like it you didn't pay. However, the clerics themselves became a bit too fond of the booze and in the eighth century the Archbishop of York banned priests from eating or drinking in taverns. In 1175 churchmen were forbidden to frequent taverns, unless on their travels.

THE SHIP

Porlock

On the main street in the village, below the notorious hill.

Porlock has a feel of splendid isolation, cut off on one side by the Bristol Channel, and on the other by the steep hills of the edge of Exmoor. It is the sort of place which requires an effort to visit, as well as good brakes. The A39 winds through the village along what was the north coast coaching route. Travelling westward, by the time the old horse-drawn coaches reached Porlock, they had already had an arduous journey and were now faced with the notorious Porlock Hill. With a gradient of 1 in 4 in places, it rises nearly 1400 feet in under three miles. A change of horses was required, not to mention a few pints of Dutch courage, and that's where the Ship Inn came in.

There had been a pub on the site for hundreds of years before the great coaching days, and an ancient window remains in the oldest part of the building. In those days, Porlock Bay saw rather more action than now. The Danes popped in every now and again during the tenth century for a bit of pillaging, and apparently in 1052 Harold, later King Harold, landed at Porlock Weir from Ireland. In view of what happened fourteen years later at Hastings, perhaps he wished he hadn't bothered.

More recently, The Ship played host to rather more peaceful customers, the literary set who, for a while, moved to enjoy the delights of Exmoor. The poets Coleridge and Southey are said to have sat in their own corner of the bar, which today looks more like a converted fireplace. They sought inspiration in the local ale, supplemented by a few pipes full of opium… allegedly!

R.D. Blackmore, whose "Lorna Doone" did for Exmoor what Wordsworth did for the Lake District, may also have supped ale in The Ship, as his hero is said to be based on a local historical character.

The bar remains much as it has been for a century or more, with good real ales on offer. But, more unusually, the pub also has its own whisky, specially blended by one of the locals who happens to be an expert professional whisky blender. Very good it is too.

Real Ales: Bass, Barn Owl, Courage.

SMITH'S ARMS

Godmanstone

On the roadside of the A352, north of Dorchester.

The fame of the Smith's Arms rests on the claim that it is the smallest pub in England, although there are one or two others which assert the same thing. I have certainly been in smaller bars, but I think it's safe to claim that the Smith's is the smallest pub building - not much bigger than a double garage.

As the name suggests, the building used to be the local blacksmith's forge. Folklore says that one day long ago Charles II was hunting in the nearby forests when he called in here to have his horse re-shod and asked the blacksmith for a little ale while he waited. On being told that the Smith had no licence to sell booze, he immediately granted him one and the place has been a pub ever since.

Nice story, but not exactly true. The correct version, apparently, is that Charles II was on the run from the Roundheads and was hidden here by the blacksmith who happened to be a keen Royalist. In return for this great favour, Charles granted him a licence, with the additional attraction of exempting him from paying tax on wines and spirits brought in from France (since most of this was probably smuggled anyway, it was no great concession).

Today the landlord of the Smith's Arms is ex-National Hunt jockey, John Foster, who, like so many in that profession, had one fall too many, and he retired to run a pub. Consequently there's a horsey feel to the place, plenty of horsey pictures around the bar and, if you eavesdrop carefully, a few good tips for the big races. I followed up one such dead certainty for the Cheltenham Gold Cup, but the money would have been much better spent on another few pints of Ringwood Bitter at the pub.

As well as a good crowd of regular locals, it's perhaps not surprising that the Smith's Arms is a tourists' honeypot, and it even welcomes the occasional coach party. Since the bar is full with just a dozen or so people, the arrival of a 50 seater coach calls for some nifty organisation, and John has it down to a fine art. They all file in through the front door and out through the back of the bar, collecting a drink on the way in a kind of factory production line, clicking away with their cameras as they shuffle forward. It is a unique entertainment which provides much amusement for the locals. When the coach parties aren't around, they tend to amuse themselves with tense games of spoof (for slugs of ouzo) and putting competitions in the bar.

Real Ales: Ringwood Best.

THE SMUGGLERS INN

SMUGGLERS INN

Osmington Mills

Turn south off the A352, Dorchester to Wareham Road at the Warmwell roundabout.

If you enjoy a quiet drink in a peaceful, uncrowded pub, avoid the Smugglers during the tourist season. It is one of the most popular spots on this stretch of coastline and visitors flock there during the summer for the fine views across to Portland. Constable's well known work, "Weymouth Bay" was painted from what is now the pub car park.

The valley up from the pub is dedicated to tourists, with the old buildings hidden now by holiday camping grounds and bungalows. It is good news for the local economy, but not so much fun if you are in search of that quiet pint.

Out of season, the pub takes on a different life and is worth a visit.

As the name suggests, this was once important smuggling territory, and the most famous of the villains was Pierre la Tour, known to all as French Peter. He used the pub as a hideaway and eventually married the landlord's daughter. Consequently, the Revenue men had a hard job catching him. One story goes that a gullible customs officer was persuaded to hide up the chimney while the landlord engaged French Peter in incriminating conversation, but the locals lit a fire and the smouldering officer fled empty-handed.

Another well known smuggler lived at Upton Fort just behind the pub. When Customs officers rushed the house they shot the poor chap who answered the door, unaware that it was the smuggler's innocent brother who just happened to be visiting at the time.

With such a history it was inevitable that the pub should be called The Smugglers Inn, but that has only happened quite recently. It was originally the Crown, and then the Picnic Inn, no doubt because the garden seems the ideal spot to enjoy a bit of al fresco eating. Local fish and lobsters are now a speciality of the house.

The pub hasn't always been welcoming to outside visitors. It used to have an old door which had a habit of swelling up when damp, making it impossible to open except by locals who knew exactly where to give it a shove. Strangers would assume the pub was closed and drive off, leaving the regular drinkers alone.

Real Ales: Dorset Best, Tanglefoot, Golden Champion, Firsty Ferret.

SQUARE & COMPASS

Worth Matravers

Signposted off the B3069 between Corfe Castle and Swanage.

This is a long way to the east of most pubs in this book, but it is well worth the journey. The Square and Compass is another of those increasingly rare gems… a proper pub which has been unaffected by the passing of the years. Serious pub hunters should not miss it.

The people of this beautiful part of Dorset have long earned their living from two main sources, fishing and stone-quarrying, and it is to the latter that this pub owes its existence. The square and compass were essential tools for the stonemason, and it was the quarrymen who were amongst the pub's best customers. In times past, they would often pay for their beer with large pieces of the local stone, which the landlord would later exchange for real money. If you ever feel your pockets are weighed down with small change, spare a thought for the poor chaps turning up at the pub with their great lumps of rock.

The pub's link with stone continues, as every year it plays host to a two-week long stone carving event, where professional and skilled amateur masons come from all over the country to produce some beautiful sculptures.

There is no bar. Drinks are served through a small hatch from a pot room at the end of the entrance corridor. It can get pretty congested. Most visitors prefer to drink on the benches outside the pub, but the weather occasionally forces them inside. There's not a lot of room but it's cosy! To the right of the corridor is a panelled room where the walls are covered with memorabilia and photos. There are reminders here of one of the pub's more distinguished guests, the artist Augustus John, who regarded it as a useful hideaway. This room is now regularly used for live music.

There is another small drinking parlour, and the third room has been converted into a fascinating museum of fossils and other bits and pieces washed up on the shores below. There aren't many pubs offering a free museum, and it is worth the trip to the Square and Compass for this alone.

For a spell during the war there was a large and top secret RAF base on the nearby headland, which provided a useful source of customers for the pub. The base was involved in developing radar, but somehow the Germans got to hear about it, and the RAF had to move out overnight. One day there were 2,000 men at the base, and the next, there was no one. Today, with the ancient Corfe Castle just up the road, this is a very popular tourist area.

Remarkably, the pub survived a spell of brewery ownership without any serious alterations, helped

largely by the fact that it has been run by the same family, the Newmans, for over a century. Present landlord, Charlie Newman, managed to buy the freehold of the pub, and he is determined to keep it just as it has always been.

Real Ales: Tanglefoot, Ringwood.

THE TROOPER

Stourton Caundle

Signposted off the A3030 about six miles east of Sherborne.

Stourton Caundle is in the heart of Dorset farming land, so it should come as no surprise that this pub has a real agricultural feel to it. The walls of the two tiny bars are covered with ancient country tools, and there are hundreds more in the well used skittle alley around the back. In other parts of the country, I have paid good money to go round rural museums with far less on display. Here, you can spend hours of fun, with pint in hand, pondering what on earth some of these strange instruments were actually used for, and there is almost certain to be a local on hand to give you a totally implausible answer. Ask about the instrument for carrying a dog... and if you believe that story, you've had one too many!

In years past, the ale houses were often to be found in farmhouses where the farmer of the day would sell home-brewed ale to supplement his income. Current landlord of The Trooper, Larry Skeats, continues this old tradition as he is a shepherd first and a publican second. A farmer all his life, he still looks after the large flocks of sheep on a nearby estate. It is Larry who has acquired all the farming bits and pieces over the past forty years or so. He also makes shepherds' crooks as a hobby, and there is a large selection of these on display in the pub. If you tire of all that, ask to see his collection of ashtrays.

Up until the Napoleonic wars the pub was called the Catherine Wheel, but it then became a centre for recruiting soldiers from the surrounding area and, in their honour, was renamed The Trooper.

Food is good, simple, basic stuff, ploughman's, toasted sandwiches etc. Larry leaves the fancy stuff to other pubs in the district, while he concentrates on the beer.

The Trooper was a favourite haunt of the late Jack Hargreaves, the first 'television countryman', whose programmes enchanted several generations. Another famous resident of Stourton Caundle was Enid Blyton, who owned the manor house opposite the pub, but nobody can remember her popping in for a drink. Not too good for the image, I suppose.

Real Ales: Champflower.

ILFRACOMBE
GRAMPUS INN
Lee
THATCHED BARN INN
Croyde
HOOPS INN
Horns Cross
COACH & HORSES
Buckland Brewer
BLACK HORSE
Great Torrington
POLTIMORE ARMS
Yarde Down
TIVERTON
DUKE OF YORK
Iddesleigh
HALF MOON INN
Sheepwash
BEER ENGINE
Newton St. Cyres
LUPPITT INN
Luppitt
TUCKERS ARMS
Dalwood
DOUBLE LOCKS
Exeter
SHIP INN
Axmouth
BRIDGE INN
Topsham
NOBODY INN
Doddiscombleigh
FOUNTAIN HEAD
Branscombe
DAWLISH
0 4 miles
0 5 kilometres

North & East Devon

BEER ENGINE

Newton St Cyres

Signposted off A377, halfway between Exeter and Crediton.

When railway lines began to carve their way through the British countryside they did, of course, have a huge effect on country pubs. Suddenly the pubs no longer had to rely on the same small group of locals. Now they had a mass of new customers transported to their door by the iron horse. This also led to new pubs being created to meet the demand.

On the outskirts of Exeter is the village of Newton St. Cyres, which found itself on the main railway line to North Devon. A pub was created here specially for these new travellers, called, imaginatively, the Railway Inn. Later it became The Old Barn Owl Inn, because the landlord had this thing about stuffed owls. Today it has returned to the railway theme neatly combined with ale, and is known as the Beer Engine. It has also reverted to the grand old tradition of brewing its own beer on the premises.

People who take beer spotting too seriously can have a lot in common with train spotters, indulging in endless monologues about the merits of one particular beer over another. It's enough to drive a man to drink something else. It follows that a pub which combines train and beer spotting could be fraught with danger, but the Beer Engine manages to avoid the trap.

Peter Hawksley, the landlord, is a man who after 20 years teaching English and Sociology decided there must be more to life, bought a rundown pub, and set up a brewery. That was 15 years ago, and Peter's beers now attract a loyal, enthusiastic and even international following. He even has a small but dedicated band of fans in France who discovered the delights of his ales when he exhibited them at a trade fair in Normandy. Anything that can encourage drinking a decent beer in France has got to be good news.

Real Ale: All Peter's beers have been named with a railway theme: Rail Ale, Piston Bitter, Sleeper Heavy, Whistlemas etc.

TALES FROM THE SNUG

In the days when all pubs and ale houses brewed their own, the towns and villages used to employ a chap who had a great job. He was called an ale connor, and he had to go round and test every new brew and make sure it was "good for men's bodies." This ale connor wore leather trousers. After tasting the brew, he would pour some of it onto a wooden seat and he would sit in the puddle of ale. If after a couple of minutes his leather trousers stuck to the seat then the brew was considered thick and sweet and alcoholic enough to pass the test. If they didn't stick it failed, and the brewer had to throw it out and start all over again. It's worth trying the experiment next time you go down to your local boozer and you think the landlord has been watering down the beer. You might get a few funny looks but it is important to maintain standards.

TALES FROM THE SNUG

Many pubs vie for the title of Britain's Oldest Pub, but it looks as if the winner is the Fighting Cocks in St Albans. This octagonal pub was built as a pigeon house in 1380, on the site of an eighth century gatehouse. Up until the seventeenth century it was a major local centre for cockfighting.

TALES FROM THE SNUG

Governments, while enjoying the revenue from alcohol duties and taxes, have always been wary of the effects of the stuff on the population. Lloyd George introduced strict opening hours during World War I as he was anxious to prevent munitions workers getting drunk. He said at the time: "We are fighting Germany, Austria and drink, and the greatest of these deadly foes is drink."

BLACK HORSE

Great Torrington

In the centre of the town.

Great Torrington had its big moment in history back in 1645 when it found itself at the centre of one of the last battles of the Civil War. Sir Thomas Fairfax , a man who knew a good thing when he saw it, set up his Parliamentarian headquarters in the Black Horse Inn. Fairfax had succeeded in taking the town from Lord Hopton's men during a battle in 1646.

Fairfax imprisoned some 200 Royalists in the church, not realising that Hopton had chosen to use the building as a powder store. The inevitable happened. There was a huge explosion, killing all the prisoners and destroying the church. In 1996 the occasion was re-enacted by enthusiastic members of the Sealed Knot who went to the trouble of building a replica of the church in order to set fire to it as the culmination of the event. Afterwards, they continued the re-enactment by quaffing large quantities of ale in the Black Horse, just as would have happened 350 years beforehand. The pub is a favourite of Sealed Knot members even when not fighting battles.

When General Fairfax and his men were in the Black Horse, there would have been no bar counter. Pot boys would have been frantically running to and from the barrels in the back trying to keep pace with the thirst. It wasn't until the early part of the 19th century that pubs started to instal a counter separating the server from the drinker. Apart from that revolutionary introduction, little else seems to have changed in the Black Horse. As well as the main bar which is generally a lively watering hole, there is a lounge and a restaurant at the back of the pub.

Real Ales: Courages, and a guest beer.

TALES FROM THE SNUG

In the days of the Civil War it was not just the quality of the ale that mattered. The style of the drinking vessel was also very important, and there were many fashinable tankards to chose from. They included: mazers, noggins, whiskins, piggins wassail-bowls, ale-bowls and jacks. Black jacks were wooden cans treated with pitch and had leather thong handles.

BRIDGE INN

Topsham

Just out of the town, on the road to Clyst St. George.

Back in Saxon times there was a wealthy chap called Toppa who set up home a few miles downstream from Exeter. It was a wise choice for a settlement, because Toppa's Ham soon became a thriving commercial port, and remained so right up until the last century. It brought huge wealth to the merchants of the area, whose grand houses can still be seen in and around the town,Topsham.

Nowadays the commercial side of the Exe estuary has almost disappeared and the place devotes itself to the leisure boaties, for whom one of the high points of the year is the annual Topsham regatta. It was Henry III who first got the town in party mood by granting a licence for a three day fair held in July.

The Bridge Inn is the oldest surviving pub in town, and it remains remarkably untouched by the passing of the beers. Parts of the building are thought to date back to the late 11th century, and it became a lodging house for the stonemasons and other craftsmen working on the building of Exeter Cathedral. Much of the material for the building would have arrived by ship up the River Exe which, incidentally, was originally named Eisca "a river abounding in fish". It's not quite like that now.

For much of the pub's history, beer was brewed on the premises, and this carried on until the turn of the century. Behind the pub is a large room which was the old malthouse and brewery. Today it has been turned into a wonderful function room which is stuck in a time warp, looking like a left over from World War II. It is filled with comfortable old furniture,the walls and shelves are stuffed full of pubabilia, and patriotic British artefacts adorn what is left of the walls and ceilings. It is used as an overflow seating area for the other tiny bars and, on occasions, a venue for live music.

The real ale tradition continues and there is always a fine selection from which to choose.

The pub has been owned by the same family for the past hundred years, and it has always been run by the women in that family. In a way, this carries on another tradition as in times past brewing was very much controlled by women. There probably wasn't enough money in it to justify the old man staying at home, so he went off in pursuit of more lucrative work, and she took care of the beer.

The Bridge became world famous in 1998 as the first British pub ever to be officially visited by Her Majesty the Queen. Her visit lasted only a few minutes as it had to be cut short because of a security alert, but it was just long enough for the Queen to accept a bottle of specially brewed beer before moving on to the next stop. The pub later received a letter to say that Prince Philip had

enjoyed it. How much more enjoyable it would have been if they had had a chance to sit down for a pie and a pint and a natter in this wonderful old pub.

Real Ales: The Bridge regularly has ten to choose from including Broadside, Summa-That, Otter, and Tanglefoot.

COACH & HORSES

Buckland Brewer

A few miles south of Bideford. Get off the main road as soon as you can and enjoy the country lanes.

Set on the top of a hill, Buckland Brewer commands wonderful views over the north Devon countryside. It is a scene of peaceful, pastoral bliss but there are one or two events in the history of the village which cast a dark shadow over the place.

The notorious Judge Jeffries is said to have stayed in the Coach & Horses on one of his trips into the

English countryside to spread terror among the local population. Research actually suggests that it is unlikely that he travelled this far west, but someone did get up to something nasty in the pub. In the ceiling of a bedroom above the bar is a sinister looking hook, and directly below that is a trap door. It appears to be a hangman's contraption, designed to send unfortunate victims to their doom.

This may account for the many ghost stories which are attached to the pub. The corner in the bar directly below the trapdoor is said to be haunted to such an extent that dogs will refuse to go there. Phantom footsteps have been heard in empty corridors upstairs, a woman in 17th century garb has been seen regularly in the bar, two cavaliers have been spotted standing in a corner, and a Roundhead has reportedly disturbed the sleep of some visitors.

These Civil War characters seem to be left over from the time when the village was at the centre of one or two major skirmishes. During renovations, a lethal canon ball was dug out of the wall of the pub and is now on display in the bar. With lumps of iron like this flying around the village, it makes you glad to have missed that particular period of history.

Despite the stories of spooks, the Coach & Horses is a friendly little pub which has been dispensing drink and hospitality to the local populace for many hundreds of years. Originally it was made up of two or three small cottages, and parts of the building date back to the 13th century. As its name suggests, it was a coaching inn for many years. Successive licensees have been kind to the old place and preserved it remarkably as it was.

Buckland Brewer is the kind of village which inspires writers. The novelist John Galsworthy lived in the area at what is now known as Galsworthy Manor, and in the early part of the ninteenth century, the village had its own famous poetic postman. Every day Edward Capern would walk the twelve mile round trip to Bideford and back, taking a rest in the village to jot down a few ballads and poems. He was so well thought of that when he retired the Prime Minister, Lord Palmerston, awarded him a pension of £50 a year.

Real Ales: Flowers Original.

DOUBLE LOCKS

Exeter

A stroll along the Exeter Canal tow-path, but best approached by boat!

One of the oldest canal-side pubs in the country, the Double Locks was built at the start of the 18th century when the canal was a busy waterway, mainly carrying wool away from Exeter, and importing a wide variety of what would then have been exotic cargoes from abroad. Olive oil came from the Mediterranean, wine from France, and salt cod from Newfoundland.

The pub was built with clinker, the material used as ballast by the sailing ships. Until quite recently, the job of publican at the Double Locks also incorporated the jobs of lock-keeper and farmer. George Tupper, who did the job for a time back in the early fifties, remembers having to leave thirsty customers in the bar every time a ship wanted to pass through the locks. He also used to keep a fine old sow which he would take to the boar for 'servicing' by means of his battered old Austin shooting-brake. The pig was a reluctant passenger on the first occasion, but soon realised the joy which waited at the end of the long journey to Crediton, and thereafter would leap into the wagon at every opportunity.

Gradually over this century, the commercial traffic has disappeared and the final nail in the coffin was the building of the motorway bridge over the canal, which prevented some of the bigger ships from getting up river. Today the canal is devoted to the pursuit of leisure. Indeed, it can be quite exhausting, sitting with a pint watching the succession of joggers and cyclists sweating their way up and down the tow-path. For the energetic imbiber, there is a pleasant day's pub crawl to be had along the canal, beginning at The Welcome Inn, moving onto the Double Locks and, finally, the Turf, before ambling back again. It's a lengthy hike, but with well-spaced out watering holes along the way.

The bar in the Double Locks is just the kind of basic, unspoilt drinking room I like. There is a smarter room at the side, but that is for eaters rather than drinkers. There is always a good selection of ales in good condition. It is an unusual pub and has become one of the 'in' places of Exeter, serving a mixed clientele of University students, locals and visitors.

Real Ales: Everard's Old Original, Abbot, Smiles and many guest ales.

TALES FROM THE SNUG

Britain's brewers produce nearly 30 million pints a day, and we drink on average 180 pints a year each. But that is less than half a pint a day. Could do better.

DUKE OF YORK

Iddesleigh

On B3217, north of Okehampton.

Dating back to the late 14th century, The Duke of York was originally four cottages built, like so many other pubs, to accommodate the craftsmen working on the church. One of these cottages later became an almshouse which, today, is the pub's dining room.

Centuries came and went and the people of Iddesleigh enjoyed a fair living from agriculture, but in the last century things went badly wrong for farmers and the population went into rapid decline. Today it is a small village of around 150 people set in the heart of beautiful rolling Devon countryside, a little bit of old England which time and most tourists pass by.

Despite its isolation, The Duke of York is a popular pub with good real ale and good food attracting those in the know from far and wide. It has also been fortunate in having a succession of good landlords, and the present incumbents, Jamie Stewart and Pippa Hutchinson, were awarded the title Licensees of the Year by the Good Pub Guide.

The big day of the year in Iddesleigh is the May Bank Holiday when the men of the Iddesleigh Friendly Society meet for their annual social get together. Once upon a time most villages had their own Friendly Society to take care of the unemployed and sick of the parish. In this age of social benefits the need for such societies has disappeared, but the tradition continues in Iddesleigh where the Society was set up in 1838. As well as being one of the few such Societies left, it is also one of the richest, but the only pay-out it makes nowadays is a few hundred pounds for funeral costs for parishioners.

On Men's Day the members of the society gather for a few drinks in the pub. Tradition decrees that they must wear a blue ribbon, and there's a fine of five pence for those who fail to do so. Having fortified themselves in the pub, members march behind the Hatherleigh Silver Band for a short service in the church, followed by a few more drinks in the pub, lunch in the village hall and an afternoon of general merry-making. The very best of old English tradition!

The late poet laureate Ted Hughes was a regular in the Duke of York, and a previous landlord was also an accomplished poet. Another famous resident of the village was the Rev Jack Russell, the hunting parson who gave his name to the terrier, and was curate here from 1830 to 1836.

Real Ales: Cotleigh, Broadside, Sharp's Doom Bar.

FOUNTAIN HEAD

Branscombe

Top end of the village, which is the next one along the coast, east of Sidmouth.

Branscombe is one of the longest villages in the country, stretching the length of a quiet east Devon valley. In a thousand years of history, Branscombe has pottered along happily without causing too much of a stir. It did have a brief moment of fame when Queen Victoria chose the lacemakers of the village and nearby Beer to produce her wedding dress, but apart from that, it has managed to stay out of the headlines.

At one end of the village is the Fountain Head, a family run pub where the landlady is Catherine Luxton. At the other is the Branscombe Vale Brewery run by Catherine's husband Graham. It is a highly convenient arrangement which ensures that the beer at the Fountain is always first class, otherwise there would be all manner of marital arguments!

I have yet to discover exactly where the 'fountain' is, but that doesn't matter. This pub is one of those rare delights, a simple watering hole which appears to have hardly changed over the 250 years it has been serving the village. The bar is plain and simple and even has... oh joy of joys... an old upright piano in one corner. On the walls are old pictures of the pub which show just how little things have changed at the Fountain Head.

One of the highspots of the year at the pub is the Beer Festival when ales are brought in from all round the country, including, of course, the Branscombe Vale own beers.

Graham Luxton and his partner Paul Dimond set up the brewery when the dairy firm they worked for closed down. It meant they could also get their hands on the dairy's stainless steel pipework which, with a bit of ingenuity, they adapted for brewing.

Few, if any breweries occupy a more attractive site. The property is owned by the National Trust and it is only a few yards from the beach, in converted stone barns. As well as supplying the Fountain Head, its beers go far and wide. It was a bottle of Branscombe's specially brewed ale which Her Majesty the Queen was given on her first ever visit to a pub, the Bridge Inn, Topsham, in 1998. Prince Philip is said to have been most appreciative.

Real Ales: Brannock, Summa-That, Olde Stoker.

TALES FROM THE SNUG

Brewers of ale on the Continent have long known the benefits of using hops in beer to act as a preservative whilst also adding taste. When hops were introduced to this country around the 14th century, it was many years before they were to be accepted. Some towns banned brewing with hops as they felt it adulterated the beer, and there were attacks on some brewers .

GRAMPUS INN

Lee

On the coast three miles to the west of Ilfracombe.

Ilfracombe gets all the attention in this part of Devon, but visitors in search of a quieter life should take a bit of time to explore some of the interesting villages in the area.

On the wild coast just three miles to the west of Ilfracombe is the little village of Lee, where for centuries the people have scratched a living from the harvest of the land and the sea, the latter occasionally providing a bonus in the shape of a shipwreck. Many vessels have met their end on the rocks of this stretch of coast, ships like the Europa, the William Wilberforce and the Lochlibo. Each tragedy brought good fortune to the village where many of the fine old buildings contain items gleaned from the wrecks.

Lee Bay was also a much-favoured landing place for smuggled spirits, much of which would have found its way to The New Inn, where the landlord was a notorious smuggler and wrecker in the 18th century. The New Inn is now the village post office. Eating and drinking has moved a short way down the road to the Grampus Inn, named after the killer whale, a creature not generally seen round these parts. What does that matter? It's a good name.

This 400 year old building used to be a farm, and more recently, a tea house. It wasn't until 1972 that it became a pub which has gained an enviable reputation in the area. There is just the one big room which serves as bar and dining room, with a welcoming fire at one end. There's regular live music here with some very talented local folk musicians.

One of the high spots of the winter is the Twelth Night celebration, with its performance of a Mummers Play and burning of the green decorations. It's all very symbolic and enjoyable.

Real Ales: Exmoor Gold, Flowers Original.

TALES FROM THE SNUG

At the turn of the century, an American writer, one Ambrose Bierce, described an abstainer as "a weak person who yields to the temptation of denying himself a pleasure."

HALF MOON INN

Sheepwash

Signposted off the A 386, just north of Hatherleigh.

Until the 18th century, Sheepwash was a bustling village at the centre of a rich agricultural area. The weekly market brought in farmers from far and near, but a fire in 1743 destroyed much of the village, and things were never the same. The market moved away, and with it the business. For a time this century the market was revived, taking place in the yard and buildings behind the pub. This was also the scene of the annual sheepdip when flocks from the surrounding area were driven into the village.

By this time, the village had been neglected by the landowner and it looked as if it would simply rot away into obscurity. However, things changed for the better when the cottages came up for private ownership, and the village was declared a conservation area. A new prosperity was born, and Sheepwash became established on the tourist trail.

You might have assumed that its unusual name owed something to all the fleecy animals decorating the fields in the area. Not so. Sheepwash is thought to derive from the Anglo Saxon 'schepewast' which, roughly speaking, meant surrounded by water. This is not exactly geographically accurate, but the River Torridge does bend round the village in the crescent shape of a half moon, which gives the pub its name.

The Half Moon dominates the attractive village square and, although records are unclear, it probably dates back to the time when it was a farmhouse/alehouse several centuries ago.
Over the years the original small inn has expanded into two other buildings along the street, one of them a school, and the other a milliner's shop.

The pub is a mecca for anglers during the trout and salmon fishing season when, of course, there is much bar talk about flies, fish and things that got away. The Half Moon also owns a long stretch of the River Torridge, and Charles Inniss, the joint landlord at the time of writing, is an experienced ghillie for guests at the pub. While he takes to the river, his brother Benji takes excellent care of the ale in the bar named after him.

It's not just visitors who are attracted to the Half Moon. Many of the locals belong to families who have lived and worked in the village for several generations and have wonderful stories to tell in rich Devon dialect.

Real Ales: Courage, Marstons Pedigree, Mainbrace.

TALES FROM THE SNUG

Back in the 17th century they didn't suffer from 'hangovers'. Instead, they woke up with a 'crapula'. A chap called Charles Cotton wrote at the time:

"The drunkard now supinely snores,
His load of ale sweats through his pores.
Yet when he wakes the swine shall find,
A crapula remains behind."

HOOPS INN

Horns Cross

On the A39 between Clovelly and Bideford.

There are many pubs in the West Country left over from the days of coaching which now seem isolated and a long way from the main tracks. The Hoops Inn, on the other hand, is a coaching inn which still looks as if it is in the right location, alongside the busy road from Barnstaple to Bideford.

It gets its name not, as you might imagine, from the metal hoop going around the coach wheel, but from the old Devon name for a bullfinch, a hoop. This area used to be great cider country, and the hills all around were covered with orchards. Sparrows and bullfinches were attracted by the apple blossom, apparently causing serious economic problems for the growers, so youngsters were paid to catch the birds. They were brought to the pub, but records don't show what happened to them after that. It's a safe bet that they weren't re-released.

Today the pub is a smart roadside inn and restaurant. It has been fairly extensively modernised but still retains large inglenook fireplaces. In an effort to recreate the days of yore, the landlord has converted what was a backroom office into a small drinkers' bar. He has done it so successfully that it looks as if it has been there for years, and it now makes a room full of 'character' in which to enjoy the many real ales on offer. There are regular beer festivals at the Hooops Inn.

Keen flyers will be interested to know that the landlord is an aircraft enthusiast with plenty of prints, paintings and models on display in the pub.

Real Ales: Local brewery and guest ales.

TALES FROM THE SNUG

It was only the well-off who could afford to travel by horse, and many roadside inn-keepers took advantage of the fact by charging extortionate amounts. The powers that be were constantly trying to curb the activities of greedy publicans. Edward III was one of those looking after the interests of the traveller when he introduced legislation against "the great and outrageous cost of victuals kept up in the realm by inn-keepers and other retailers of victuals, to the great detriment of the people travelling over the country."

LUPPITT INN

Luppitt

To the north of Honiton, signposted off by-pass.

Antique collectors get it when they find a rare bargain. Gamblers get it with the jackpot. Fishermen get it when they land the big one, and pub hunters get it when they stumble across a place like The Luppitt Inn.

This is closer to the traditional English country pub than anything dreamt up by brewery advertising men. For hundreds of years, life in the English countryside was tough. Farmers and farm labourers worked long, hard hours trying to earn an honest crust, and many of them had a wife at home who would try to supplement the meagre income by brewing ale and selling it on to thirsty visitors. They didn't need fancy wooden bars, collections of antique brasses, and hunting prints. They managed by selling good beer from their front rooms or parlours, and that is exactly what the Luppitt Inn does today, seemingly uninfluenced by modern pub trends.

If all those worthies running conservation, restoration and preservation quangoes had any sense, they would ensure that The Luppitt was protected for the nation.

The pub is only a few miles from the rush of the traffic on the A303, but Luppitt has that feel of being in a world and time scale of its own. It is Shangri La, with the Inn at one end of the village, and a brewery at the other. In short, a pub lover's dream come true.

The Luppitt Inn is little more than a front room in the old stone farmhouse. It is still very much a working farm and the car park is shared with assorted chickens, cats, and, occasionally, inquisitive cows. Landlady Mary Wright runs the place more for love than profit, and, in return, she is much-loved by the village regulars. Mary came to Luppitt during the war when she married Albie Wright. It was a busy time in the village, as just up the road was Dunkerswell airfield, the base for many thirsty American servicemen.

The pub is not always open, but a knock on the stable door usually brings a response and Mary will welcome customers into the tiny bar. There are bench seats, enough for half a dozen or so, at one side, and at the other a couple of barrels of local Otter beer with a few spirits on sale as well. Food is limited to packets of crisps and nuts. In the event of a rush, there is another small overflow room with simple tables and chairs, and even a dartboard.

On the walls of the bar are dozens of old photographs depicting life in Luppitt many decades ago, but amongst the faded prints is a raunchy picture of Tina Turner signed, " With love to all at the Luppitt, Love Tina." You never know who you're going to meet in some of these places!

Real Ales: Otter Best.

NOBODY INN

Doddiscombleigh

Signposted from the B3193 Teign Valley road.

Not so long ago, nipping down to the local meant going for a drink, a chat with a few mates, and a game of darts perhaps, but first and foremost, a drink. If you felt peckish, you were lucky to get so much as a sausage on a stick or a pickled egg, or for something really exotic, smokey bacon flavoured crisps. All that has changed.

Nowadays, more and more country pubs are having to turn to food in order to attract the customers out of the towns. So much so, that I'm told we're spending 4.8 billion pounds a year on pub food. Now that's equivalent to the gross domestic product of a place like Iceland. It's petty cash to Bill Gates, but it's a lot of money to publicans.

Too many pubs have turned into restaurants which just happen to sell drinks, rather than the other way round. For those, like me, who happen to enjoy a pint without plates full of scampi and chips being constantly passed under the nose, it's a regrettable trend.

The Nobody Inn at Doddiscombleigh somehow manages to combine the interests of both eaters and drinkers without making either group feel uncomfortable. The food is special, and goes way beyond the usual pub menu that seems to be replicated throughout the country. Foodies enjoy this pub. Even non foodies, like me (it's not good to put solids in a hydraulic system!) can find much to appreciate, not least from a cheese board which boasts 40 West Country cheeses.

For the drinkers, who can argue with a pub that has three good real ales (Nobody Bitter, Cotleigh Tawny and Bass) and a wine list that features 800 wines? It will take you most of the day just to read the list, so don't go to the Nobody Inn if you're in a hurry. As if all this is not enough, landlord Nick Borst Smith also specialises in whisky, with 250 brands on offer. In spite of this, he still gets the whisky bores coming in, ordering a particularly obscure highland malt by name, and then drowning it with ginger ale.

The Nobody Inn is a 12th century building retaining its original beams and inglenook fireplace. It used to be called the New Inn, and there are a couple of different stories about how it got its present name. One refers to a mix-up following the death of a previous landlord. After his coffin was buried in the church next to the pub, a call from the undertaker revealed that they'd somehow forgotten to put the poor man's body in it - No Body In the coffin. Another suggests that there was once a rather grumpy landlord of the pub who did not like serving the local riff raff. When one would knock on the door in the hope of a drink, he would shout that there was "Nobody In, so go away".

Whatever the truth, its a pub which is well worth seeking out.

Beers: Nobody Bitter, Cotleigh Tawny, Bass.

TALES FROM THE SNUG

Amongst drinkers the national emblem of Ireland is Guinness, and there are endless conversations about the difference in taste between Irish Guinness and the same drink in England. Yet Guinness began life as a very English type of beer, and owes its origins to 'porter' which was first brewed in London early in the eighteenth century. In those days it was very popular with working men and its popularity spread throughout the land, including Ireland. For some reason it fell out of favour in mainland Britain, but the Irish never lost their passion for the drink and, in 1799, Arthur Guinness's Brewery in Dublin devoted itself to the dark brew. He made a fortune by selling it back to the English as a 'stout' an apt name given to full-bodied beers.

TALES FROM THE SNUG

"When you have lost your inns, drown your empty selves, for you will have lost the last of England." (Hilaire Belloc)

TALES FROM THE SNUG

Many drinkers firmly believe that "a little of what you fancy does you good", and will argue about the health-giving qualities of their chosen tipple. Cider drinkers of a bygone age believed it was a good cure for gout, rheumatism and all manner of other afflictions. Captain Cook took cider with him on his voyages of discovery to help ward off scurvy. Others believed that a paste made up from cider apple pulp and pig fat was good for the complexion.

POLTIMORE ARMS

Yarde Down

Part of the fun of this place is trying to find it. To make it easier, take the A399 at Blackmoor Gate on the A361 Tiverton to Barnstaple road. One mile after the roundabout take the Simonsbath road and, with luck, you should find the pub 4 miles down that road.

For pub hunters with a passion for real, totally unspoilt watering holes, it is hard to beat the Poltimore Arms.

Many landlords of country pubs are finding it increasingly difficult to earn a reasonable living. They blame everything from high duties on alcohol to tougher drink-drive laws, but I suspect that in many cases, the pubs are unsuccessful simply because they are not very good landlords. For an example of how a country pub can succeed against all the odds, they should pop into the Poltimore Arms.

The Poltimore has no electricity, no gas, no mains water, and, because there are no houses within miles, you would expect it to have no customers either. On the contrary. The pub does a good, steady trade, and those in the know travel from miles around (they have to) to enjoy it.

Very little has changed here in the past three hundred years, except that the bar has been extended slightly and is now all of about three feet long. It used to be an even smaller serving hatch. Apart from that, the pub remains just as it must have been during the Civil War, when the canny landlord managed to appeal to both Parliamentarians and Royalists. For a couple of centuries after that it was a successful staging post for the horse traffic of Exmoor.

Today, because of its remoteness, it is the kind of pub that strangers simply stumble upon by accident. Most of its locals are the hill farmers of the western part of the moor, and three times a year there is a traditional Sheep Fair in the field opposite the pub. Such fairs are rapidly dying out, as most farmers tend to use the big markets instead, but in this part of Devon the old ways happily continue.

In spite of its lack of basic amenities, the pub has a justifiably excellent reputation for its food. Power comes from a generator in the garage, with a bit of bottled gas to help out, and water comes from a bore-hole up the hill. With this combination, Dawn in the kitchen turns out some delicious and surprisingly exotic dishes, while Richard in the bar serves a fine drop of local beer.

The Poltimore is in a beautiful part of the country, and I have been lucky in that whenever I have been to the pub it has been a fine, sunny day. I gather that this is the exception rather than the rule though, and things can be a bit wet and bleak here. Consequently, (be warned) in the middle of winter the pub may not be open every lunchtime.

For those susceptible to such things, the pub does have its resident ghost which specialises in various poltergeistic activities such as turning pictures upside down and making empty copper kettles whistle. Whoever or whatever it is, it does not affect the friendly atmosphere in the simple small bar.

The Poltimore Arms is a gem.

REAL ALES: Cotleigh.

SHIP INN

Axmouth

On the road into the village.

That famous Roman road, the Foss Way, is generally thought to run from Exeter to Lincoln, but there are those who believe that Axmouth is the southern end of the route. Whatever the truth, it is likely that the odd Legion or two did arrive in the port and that, somehow, they connected up with the route north. It is also probable that, having arrived in this little port, the Italian visitors would have set up one of their infamous tavernas, since apparently they could not travel far without an infusion of plonk to remind them of home.

These tavernas were the 2000 year old equivalent of motorway services, but the food was probably better, and you didn 't have to queue for the loo. The ancient Brits quite liked the new idea. It's not recorded where we did our drinking before then. No doubt we just drifted from mud hut to mud hut hoping to find a neighbour with a fresh brew of ale on the go. For some reason the thought of having special places where we could all gather together for a convivial drink had never occurred to us.

Exactly where in Axmouth the Roman taverna might have been has been lost in the mists of history but there is, at least, a record dating back a thousand years to show that there was an ale-house on the site of what is now the Ship Inn. It is thought to have been where the pub's skittle alley is today.

When a pub has been under the same family ownership for many years, you know you are on to a good thing, and it is reassuring to discover that the current owners of the Ship, the Chapmans, have been there for a long time. After all, nobody survives for long in the business if they run a rotten pub. The fact that Christopher Chapman is the son of Fanny Craddock, the first queen of telly-chefs, also ensures that the food is different from the average pub fare.

The whole family has been seriously afflicted with the collecting bug - stamps, Garfield ephemera, dolls, and anything to do with Guinness. The dolls, collected from around the world, are in display cases in the bars and dining area, and the Guinness collection has a special bar of its own. Any fan of the Black Stuff will be able to enjoy an hour or two examining the Guinness mugs, ashtrays, ties, toucans and other paraphernalia which cover the walls. The proprietors also serve a very decent pint of the stuff. A hundred years ago the Ship almost disappeared for ever when the local fire brigade refused to put out a blaze in the pub, and it was largely destroyed. Fortunately it was rebuilt, and now enjoys an excellent reputation in this popular coastal area of East Devon.

Real Ales: Bass, Otter, Flowers (and, of course, Guinness).

TALES FROM THE SNUG

In ancient Rome, wine was considered a product of the Gods. It was so precious that no-one under the age of thirty and no women or servants were allowed to touch the stuff. Romulus, the founder of Rome, laid down a law allowing a husband to execute his wife for two sins: adultery and drinking wine. And it became a custom for the men to kiss women on the lips to see if they'd been at the bottle.

THATCHED BARN INN

Croyde

Straight on through Braunton on the B3231. When the road runs out, you're there.

We know that the art of making ale goes back at least 3000 years, but I like to think that way back in the Stone Age, it was purely by accident that man discovered that grain or fruit left in a pot of water eventually flavoured that water, and gave it a strength which had a remarkable affect on the head. The process of fermentaion was no doubt beyond their comprehension, but I am sure they enjoyed its results, which would have brightened up life around the campfire.

They weren't stupid, these Stone Age people. They knew a good site to set up home for a start, and some of them chose the area around Croyde. On two sides, it is cut off from the rest of the country by Dartmoor and Exmoor, and on the other two sides it has the sea - a fairly safe place to set up home, with barriers on all sides to deter all but the most determined invader. This is where the Vikings come into the story.

One of the big cheeses in the Viking world was a certain Lord Crydda, who landed here with a bunch of his fellow hooligans, intent on a bit of rape and pillage. He named the place after himself. For a thousand years afterwards, Croyde managed to repel all other invaders, until the coming of the railways and the horseless carriage brought Edwardian tourists to the area, beginning a new prosperous life for the town.

The Thatched Barn Inn is a late twentieth century pub, cunningly concealed by ancient clothing. From the outside it is plain to see that the building dates back at least four centuries, but the inside has been brought up to date to cater for modern demands. However, while one section is turned over to eaters, there is still a good bar for more liquid pursuits.

Back in the 16th century the place was little more than a barn for animals. After that it had many uses over the years, but most recently it had been a restaurant, tea-room and shop. It wasn't until 1978 that it became a pub, and it has now grown into a successful business, attracting locals and tourists alike.

During the season it is a very popular watering hole, and one of its busiest times is around the Viking Festival in June when Lord Crydda is remembered by the locals dressing up in appropriate garb. Nowadays the rape and pillage bit is actively discouraged.

REAL ALES: Hicks Special Draft, Bass, local guest ales.

TUCKERS ARMS

Dalwood

North of the A35, about halfway between Honiton and Axminster.

During the time when the Romans were making themselves unwelcome in our land, the Axe Valley would have seen a lot of activity as one of their main thoroughfares. Since they had a reputation for not travelling too far without a stop for a glass of wine, they probably established a taverna or two round about Dalwood.

That, though, is just speculation. What we do know is that the Tuckers Arms dates back to the time of the building of the church, between the 13th and 15th centuries. It stands on land donated to the village by no less a benefactor than William the Conqueror, and it was used as a hunting lodge for the great and good of the land, including the Dukes of Beaulieu. The ceilings in the main bar show that, at this stage, there was a balcony which would have served as a sleeping area. During the 15th century the building served as a farmhouse, and from that period there remains a passage from the back to the front of the building.

Edward III granted the village the right to hold an annual fair which, apart from a time in the last century, has been the main event in the village's social calendar, although May Day celebrations outside the pub come a close second.

Dalwood has always been at the centre of a thriving farming community with mills for corn, malt and wool. There was also good business to be had from soap-boiling, and tanning.

For many years the pub was called the New Inn, like so many others, but in 1834 it was taken over by a Mr William Tucker of Kilmington who must have had something of an ego problem, since he promptly renamed it after himself.

Real Ales: Otter, Flowers Original.

TALES FROM THE SNUG

In early days, the strength of a spirit was tested by pouring a tot of the stuff onto some gunpowder and setting fire to it. If it was a strong proof spirit, the liquid would burn away and the gunpowder would ignite. If it was under proof, the water remaining would prevent the firing of the powder. This method is not recommended today, even if you suspect that your whisky has been watered down. Modern landlords tend to take a dim view of the practice.

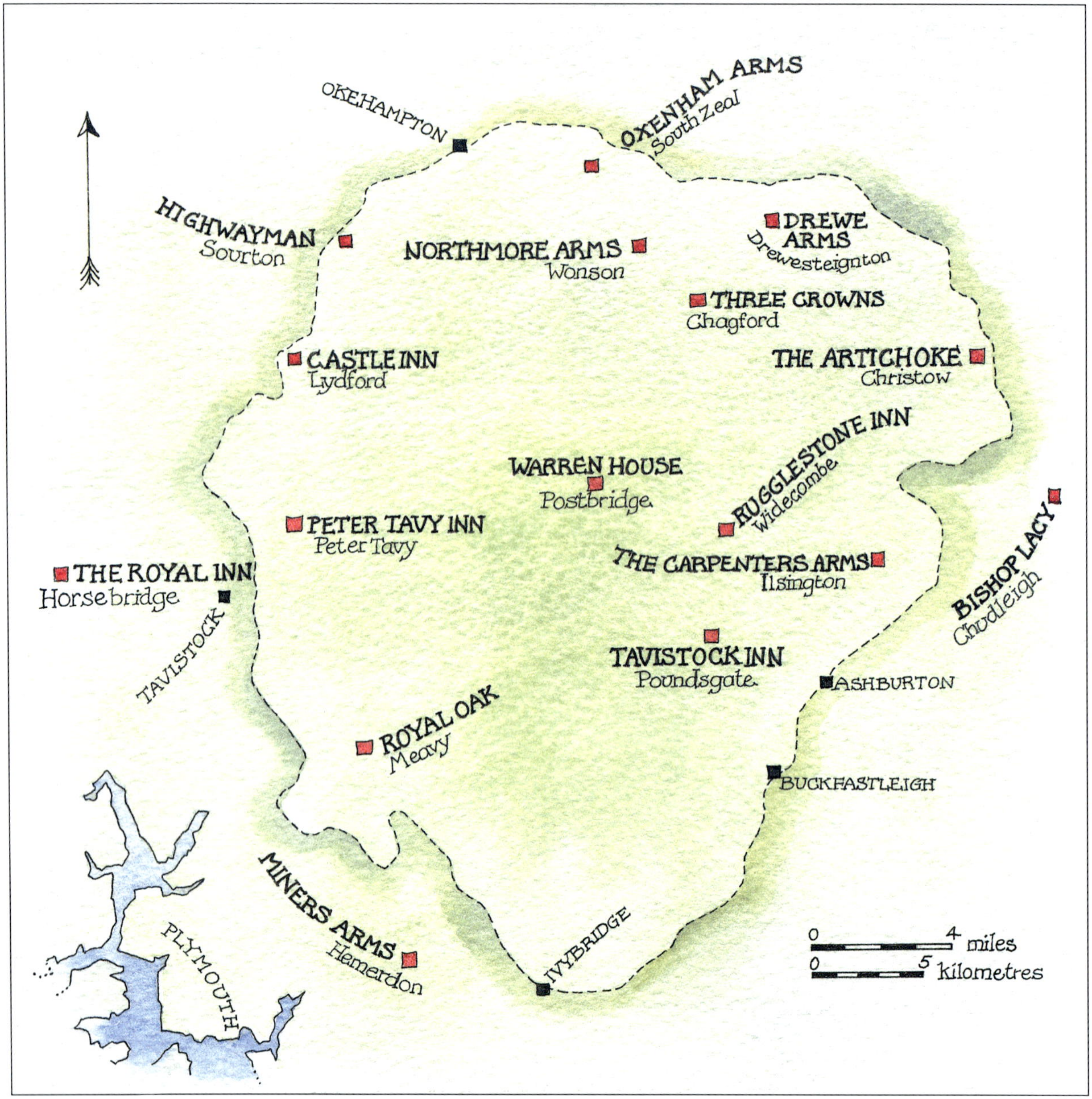
OKEHAMPTON
OXENHAM ARMS
South Zeal
HIGHWAYMAN
Sourton
NORTHMORE ARMS
Wonson
DREWE ARMS
Drewesteignton
THREE CROWNS
Chagford
CASTLE INN
Lydford
THE ARTICHOKE
Christow
RUGGLESTONE INN
Widecombe
WARREN HOUSE
Postbridge
PETER TAVY INN
Peter Tavy
THE ROYAL INN
Horsebridge
THE CARPENTERS ARMS
Ilsington
BISHOP LACY
Chudleigh
TAVISTOCK
TAVISTOCK INN
Poundsgate
ASHBURTON
ROYAL OAK
Meavy
BUCKFASTLEIGH
MINERS ARMS
Hemerdon
IVYBRIDGE
PLYMOUTH
0 4 miles
0 5 kilometres

Dartmoor & Surrounds

THE ARTICHOKE

Christow

Drive north up the Teign Valley and Christow is tucked away up a narrow lane to the left.

Imagine popping down to the Brussel Sprout for a quick one, or having a noggin in the Red Cabbage. There can't be many pubs named after a vegetable, but back in the times of the Crusades, they decided to build a pub in Christow and call it The Artichoke, since Jerusalem artichokes are what the brave crusaders brought back from their travels. They also, no doubt, brought back stuffed fluffy camels, a souvenir fez and raffia table mats, but fortunately they were ignored when it came to the pub-naming.

Landowners at the time were required by law to provide a percentage of their workforce to join the Crusades. In Christow they hung an artichoke outside the ale-house and used it as a recruiting centre for the unfortunate men who had, no doubt, been forcibly 'volunteered'.

This beautiful part of Devon has been attracting residents since the Bronze Age and the remains of their hut circles can still be seen above the present day village. Not much happened in Christow for hundreds of years but then they discovered lead, zinc and silver which precipitated a mining boom in the area. For many years the village thrived and prospered, but now all that remains of the industry are a few derelict buildings and chimneys and, down the valley, some unsightly slag heaps rich in arsenic deposits.

On a more romantic note, Christow achieved national recognition through the author and broadcaster, Arthur Marshall, who lived there and wrote about his life in the village which he re-christened "Myrtle Bank".

The pub has carried on business in the centre of the village throughout all the fluctuations in the local economy. In the early days it brewed its own ale, making use of water from the moorland stream which still runs through the small garden. The Artichoke is small (but perfectly formed) with room for only half a dozen drinkers at the bar. Up a few steps is another small room which still features a high bench used by crusading warriors. It had to be high in order for them to sit down while still wearing their swords.

Real Ales: Bass.

TALES FROM THE SNUG

The Crusades saw the start of a worrying trend. Whenever Governments found themselves a bit short of the readies to pay for a war, they found an easy way of raising money was to tax the poor drinker. Henry II started it by slapping a tax on ale in 1188 called the Saladin Tithe, to finance the Crusades.

BISHOP LACY

Chudleigh

On the main street opposite the church.

This, like so many pubs in the West Country, is set on the busy main street of a market town with no obvious place to park the car. Consequently many people rush on by and miss a treat.

Two-thirds of Chudleigh was destroyed in a great fire of 1807 which raged through the market town. At the height of the fire the townsfolk rushed to place many of their smouldering possessions in the safety of the newly built brick and slate Market Hall, unaware that the Hall was also being used to store gunpowder for the local quarry. The inevitable happened and the whole thing blew up with a bang, which apparently scattered the contents across a two mile radius. Remarkably, the only casualties of the fire were a pig and a horse, but nearly a thousand people were made homeless.

The fire burned fiercely until confronted by the wall of the pub, where it came to a halt, leaving the ancient building comparatively unscathed.

The Bishop Lacy is one of those church house pubs, built for the church masons, and a tunnel is said to run between it and the church opposite. Many pubs claim similar tunnels, but I haven't actually seen one yet! It used to be called the Plymouth Inn, but was renamed after the much loved Bishop Edmund Lacy, the Bishop of Exeter from 1420 to 1455, who spent as much time as possible in the Bishop's Palace in Chudleigh. He brought fresh water to the village by means of a brilliantly constructed leat from the top of Haldon Hill. This split into two when it reached Chudleigh, one part supplying the villagers, with 'dipping' spots for them to draw the much needed water, and the other part ending up in the Bishop's garden where it provided a constant top-up for his prize fishpond.

The pub went through a bad patch, but current licensees Robin and Wendy Bishop (no relation to old Lacy) have restored it to its former glory, with a thriving local trade. Although comparatively new to the trade, they know the importance of providing good beer and food and looking after the locals, and they have resisted the temptation to make any drastic alterations to the structure of the place. They also get a lot of fun out of the job. Wendy's laugh is infectious, but any resemblance between it and Sybil's guffaw in Fawlty Towers, is purely coincidental!

Real Ales: Jail Ale, Branscombe, Bishop's Beauty. Guest Ales.

THE CARPENTERS ARMS

Ilsington

Signposted off the A38 at Bovey Tracey roundabout.

Ilsington is one of the largest parishes in Devon, stretching from the Trago Mills complex in the south, to Haytor in the north. At its centre is the small, but perfectly formed, village of Ilsington itself, and at the centre of Ilsington is this 'proper' pub, the Carpenters.

Unlike some other pubs in this area, the Carpenters does not aim itself at the tourist market (although visitors are made more than welcome). Set back from the main road in the village, most traffic passes straight through. There used to be a signpost to the Carpenters, but some bright spark pinched it, leaving the pub hidden from all but those in the know.

It is now what it always has been, a village local, catering primarily for a good bunch of regulars. It's believed that it was once a farm house forming part of the local estate. The earliest reference to it being a pub is in the early 1800s, although there seems little doubt that it was providing beer for the local population long before that.

Today the Carpenters Arms offers good beer, served straight from the barrel, good basic food, a welcoming fire in the winter, and a landlord and landlady who care about their customers. There is even a wonderful tiny serving hatch through to the back passage, through which the village children buy their supplies of sweets and chocolates. Cigarettes and tobacco are served from the bar rather than from one of those infernal slot machines. A small point, but I am paranoid about these automatic dispensers in pubs. It's only a matter of time before someone comes up with a coin-in-the-slot beer dispenser, which will be another nail in the coffin of The Local.

The Carpenters is exactly what village pubs should be, the centre of the community. For a small village it is remarkable how much goes on, and all activities seem to involve the pub. As well as a keen darts team… keen, but not too serious… there's a bowls team and an 'international' football team, Ilsington Villa.

The players of Ilsington Villa once went on a bit of a jolly to Gambia, where they were confronted with rather more than they bargained for. A breakdown in communications somewhere meant that the Gambian authorities thought it was Aston Villa who had come for a game. They recalled all their overseas players, and the Ilsington lads found themselves with a match against the Gambian national team in the national stadium, complete with all the marching bands and official receptions. They acquitted themselves quite well, being beaten by a mere nine goals to nil.

Real Ales: Flowers, Old Speckled Hen.

TALES FROM THE SNUG

Brewing and selling ale to the neighbours was always a useful way of bringing a few more pennies into the household. The ballad of Industrious Smith, published during the reign of Charles I records the efforts of one such brewer:

"I see by my labour but little I thrive
And that against the stream I do strive
By selling of ale some money is got
If every man honestly pay for his pot
By this we may keep the wolf from the door."

CASTLE INN

Lydford

Signposted to the west of the A386, half way between Tavistock and Okehampton.

It's strange how nowadays pubs provide so much pleasure and enjoyment for so many people when not so long ago some of them were also used for the administration of misery and even death. The Castle Inn at Lydford is one such place. It was here that the great and the good and even, according to the stories, the notorious Judge Jeffries himself, would have stayed and sat in judgement over lesser mortals. If they were really unlucky they would have ended up next door, in the keep of the Norman

Castle where over the centuries hundreds of prisoners were incarcerated and executed. The cruel goings-on here were known throughout the county. There was a local poet, a chap called William Brown, who wrote a ballad about the place:

I oft heard of Lydford Law
Where in the morning they hang and draw
And sit in judgement after.

The last execution in Lydford was in 1650 at a time when the village was described as "mean and miserable." Today it's a popular spot on the Dartmoor tourist map, and at the heart of the village is the Castle Inn which manages still to feel like a village pub at the same time as being a well-renowned restaurant and hotel. It is also a pub which is proud of its history.

A thousand years ago Lydford was one of several places throughout the land where Ethelred the Unready decided to set up a mint. The trouble with having a mint in town is that it attracts all sorts of nasty visitors intent on helping themselves, and so it was that the Vikings visited Lydford for a bit of pillaging. It must have come as a pleasant surprise to them to discover so much wealth in such a remote Dartmoor village. Of the Lydford coins still in existence two are in the British Museum, there are a couple on the wall of the Castle Inn and the rest are in Denmark. Forget the Elgin Marbles. Lydford wants its pennies back.

Needless to say, the Castle boasts a few non-paying residents in the form of ghostly apparitions which occasionally appear to even the most sceptical of visitors. A London taxi driver (a breed not normally known for their susceptibility to things supernatural) recently cut short his stay when confronted with the spectre of an elderly grey-haired man hovering in the bar. Next door in the Castle Keep the ghost of some poor soul in history takes the form of a black pig.

It's thought the pub started out as the Keeper of the Castle's house. Over the years the Castle Inn has undergone its fair share of refurbishment, redecoration and addition, but it has been done carefully to retain the character of the old building. They must have done it well as it also manages to retain a good crowd of loyal locals.

Real Ales: London Pride, Blackawton.

TALES FROM THE SNUG

When the Romans left (not before time) the British decided that their tavernas were not a bad idea. We weren't too keen on all that cheap Italian plonk, but the idea of having roadside drinking houses had, for some reason, never occured to us. We adapted them into the forerunners of today's pubs. Since, at the time, not many people could read or write, there was little point having a notice outside these establishments, so instead they were marked with a long pole, or ale-stake, which poked out into the road - taking the unwary horsemen by surprise.

DREWE ARMS

Drewsteignton

Signposted off the A382 between Moretonhampstead and Okehampton.

This pub became famous for being the domain of the country's longest serving landladies, Mabel Mudge. As a result, most locals still refer to it as Aunty Mabel's rather than the Drewe Arms, which is not exactly what Julius Drewe had in mind.

Mr. Drewe made a fortune from tea and founding Home and Colonial Stores. He was so rich that he retired at the age of thirty-three and scoured the country for a place to settle down for the rest of his life. He believed that the Drew bit of Drewsteignton was a family connection dating back hundreds of years, and this prompted him to put down his roots here. He did so in grand style by commissioning Edwin Lutyens to design a castle for him. The building of his Castle Drogo kept the men of the village in work for many years, and it was a busy time for the pub. At that stage it was called the Druids Arms, but Mr Drewe made the brewery an offer of 'one of the best inn signs in the land' in exchange for re-naming the pub.

Aunty Mabel was landlady here for seventy-five years, eventually leaving to move into a home at the age of ninety-nine. She died two years later, and is still remembered with great affection by the villagers of Drewsteignton. Throughout her life at the pub the Whitbread Brewery, very wisely, allowed her to run it in her own inimitable way, without insisting on any of the modernisation which was applied to their other pubs. Even when she was growing frail the brewery allowed her to stay on, and the locals helped out with the work. So, big breweries are not always the villains they are made out to be!

When Mabel left there were fears that the old place would be changed, and the villagers organised a 'Save the Drewe' campaign which even attracted national interest. The members of the group ran the place themselves for nearly a year. So strong were the feelings that when a new tenant moved in, very little changed.

Food used to be restricted to sandwiches and a ploughman's lunch, but now one room has been opened up as a dining area for a much wider range. Apart from that, the Drewe Arms is still very much as it was during Mabel's days, a delightful old and basic country inn.

Real Ales: Bass, Marston's Pedigree, Old Speckled Hen.

HIGHWAYMAN

Sourton

A few miles south of Okehampton on the A386.

I am not, as you may have gathered, a great fan of pubs which have been tarted up, prettified, converted into eateries, or otherwise messed about with. Consequently, although I have driven up and down the A386 many times, I always rushed past The Highwayman at Sourton which, from the road, appears like something dreamt up by a Walt Disney designer on an hallucinogenic drug. It's an old farmhouse decorated in a manner which can only be described as bizarre.

Overcome by thirst one day, I ignored my prejudices and went inside, where things are even more bizarre. Much to my surprise, I liked it.

The Highwayman is like no other pub I have come across. One small bar and dining room is a re-creation of a sailing ship's cabin, with one or two authentic bits and pieces from real ships, and a few cunningly created driftwood sculptures. Another corner is transformed into a forest glade grotto, complete with a variety of stuffed animals, and a glass floor imported from a Plymouth Almshouse.

Customers here need never get bored, there are bits and pieces to be identified wherever you look. There's a strange machine for pushing pills down a horse's throat, antique spinning wheels and cider presses, and an intriguing device used by wartime aircrews who were often stuck for hours in an aircraft with no loo!

This transformation has happened gradually over the past 40 years thanks to the vivid imagination of Buster and Rita Jones, who have just retired, leaving the pub in the hands of their daughter, Sally.

Originally the pub was one of the thousands of New Inns created during the reign of Elizabeth I, and it survived for many years as a farmhouse pub. This stretch of road used to be the workplace of three notorious highwaymen and it was after them that the pub was renamed. Strange how villains acquire a kind of romance with the passage of time. Perhaps in a few centuries time we shall see a crop of pubs called The Mugger, or the Armed Robber, or the Computer Fraudster.

The Highwayman is everything I ought to dislike about refurbished pubs, but it's so odd, its wonderful!

Real Ales: Flowers Best.

TALES FROM THE SNUG

Ale has long been seen as a source of inspiration for artists and writers. The English writer Thomas Moore wrote 150 years ago:

"If with water you fill up your glasses
You'll never write anything wise.
For ale is the horse of Parnassus
Which hurries a bard to the skies."

MINERS ARMS

Hemerdon

Through Plympton, past the Newnham Industrial Estate and, before you know it, you're in the countryside and in the hamlet of Hemerdon.

If I had to compile a list of my favourite pubs, the Miners would be very near the top. I must admit a certain bias here as I have been known to pop in for a quick half on more than one occasion.

It is my sort of pub. The first time I drank in the Miners, the chimney caught fire and the bar filled with smoke and sparks. None of the locals moved except to place a hand over the top of their pints to protect them from the falling soot. Drinking just carried on as if nothing had happened. In Hemerdon, beer is taken seriously and nothing gets in the way of its enjoyment.

Many pubs today are little more than eating houses which just happen to serve beer. Old bar-rooms full of character and atmosphere have been converted into smart dining areas which all look basically the same and offer almost identical dishes. There is food at the Miners Arms but it is simple fare ranging from toasted sandwiches to cottage pie. Also (and this is a very good sign) pickled eggs! You don't see those too often nowadays.

Landlords come and landlords go, and just a few stay on for ever. The licence at the Miners Arms has been in the Honey family since the pub was opened early last century. But it wasn't until after the war that the family actually bought the pub. After all those years in the business the Honeys know a thing or two about running a good pub.

It began life three hundred years ago as a farmhouse. Spotting a chance to make an extra penny or two the Honey ancestors started supplying cider to the miners working at nearby Bottle Hill, but inadvertently forgot to apply for a licence. When the Customs and Excise man caught up with them, he was fobbed off with a bribe of hay for his horse and he went back to Plymouth without prosecuting. After that it was decided to legalise the trade and the Miners Arms was born as a proper pub.

Mining for tin and tungsten had been the main activity in the hamlet of Hemerdon and, although the mines closed down many years ago, old bits of mining equipment still adorn the pub today. There are three drinking areas to suit every mood: a proper drinkers bar, an adjoining room for more private goings-on and a smart 'lounge' bar at the back which features the original well that once served the pub.

The City of Plymouth is just down the road, but the Miners still retains its character as a proper pub which feels as if it is buried deep in the Devon countryside.

Real Ales: Bass, on pump and direct from the barrel; Suttons XSB and a regular guest ale.

NORTHMORE ARMS

Wonson

A couple of miles south west of Whiddon Down on the A382, start exploring the lanes with a good map.

Amongst the many well worn paths across Dartmoor, there's one called the Mariner's Way. Life was tough for sailors, and often they would leave a ship in a south Devon port and have to seek work on another one on the north coast, or vice versa. This was in the days when the public transport system was about on the same level as it is today. So, in the absence of motor vehicles, there was only one way to get to the next job, walk - a hundred mile hike across the wild moors. Today, hundreds of walkers every year do the route through wild, ancient landscapes and lush valleys just for the pleasure. Personally I prefer to do it in my old Doris.

Along the route is the village of Throwleigh, which is one of those off the beaten track places most motorists just happen to find by accident, but it's definitely worth seeking out, and not just because it's a pretty little place. There also happens to be a darn good pub in the nearby hamlet of Wonson.

Pub hunting for me has been a life-long hobby. It's been a kind of mission almost, seeking out that perfect watering hole, the quest for the holy ale. Though I've never actually been bird watching, I imagine it's quite similar… that great thrill when you find a rare specimen. In my case that means an unspoilt pub serving good beer, good food, and good company. The Northmore Arms is one such specimen.

It was probably set up by some enterprising farmer who thought he would convert a room on the side into an ale-house to cater for the walk-weary mariners on their hundred mile march across the county. One of those original customers seems to have liked the place so much he stayed, as the ghost of an old mariner is sometimes seen sitting beside the fire, or so they say.

The Northmore remains what so many pubs used to be, a small farmhouse front room serving beer. No frills, no gimmicks. There's also good, simple food. The elusive steak and kidney pudding can be found here - not the pie, but the pudding, which is getting increasingly difficult to find on pub menus.

The Northmore Arms is one of those pubs you only stumble across if you're lost but, if you're going to get lost, I can think of no better place to do it in. This is in the heart of farming country and while most visitors to the pub have got there more or less by accident, it's also well used by the locals, and a lot of the farmers I know round there are quite keen on the odd snifter. When the Dartmoor mist sets in and one of them sets off in search of a missing ewe, it's not uncommon for him to pop in to the Northmore for a quick reviver, and to find himself settled in for the rest of the day.

Another good thing about a country pub like this is that it is immune from some of the commercial pressures which have ruined so many other pubs in country areas. There is no point in installing juke boxes, fruit machines, automated beer pumps and the like. To do so would kill the local trade and, in a pub which is off the beaten tourist track, that would quickly mean death for the whole place.

Most of the land around the Northmore Arms once belonged to said Northmore who was a keen gambler. Keen, but not very good. In one game he gambled his entire 60,000 acre estate, and lost the lot on the turn of a card.

REAL ALES: Cotleigh Tawny, Exe Valley Dobs, Adnams Broadside.

TALES FROM THE SNUG

In the 13th century the powers that be grew increasingly worried about the rocketing price of ale and attempted to peg the price to the price of grain. In towns it was fixed at a halfpenny a gallon, and in rural areas it was about a farthing. So in the countryside one new penny would have bought you around nine gallons of beer.

OXENHAM ARMS

South Zeal

In the main street of South Zeal, near Okehampton.

This is another of those magnificent houses, built of the finest granite to last for ever. The Oxenham Arms dominates the quiet main street of South Zeal, and is a reminder of the prosperity which the area used to enjoy as a centre of the woollen industry.

Many pubs claim to have parts of the building dating back a few centuries, but the Oxenham Arms tops them all. The centrepiece of a room behind the bar is a mystical monolith which has been in position for 5000 years. Various interested parties have dug as deep as they can around the stone, but its foundations have never been reached. Others have found evidence of magnetic forces, ley lines, and, for all I know, corn circles and alien civilisations.

All this is of little importance to those who pop into the Oxenham Arms for a quick drink, but it does tend to suggest that the building is on a site where people have gathered for a handful of millenia and, no doubt, enjoyed a pot or two of loopy juice as they did so. The history of drinking at the Oxenham probably goes back a long way.

Whether or not they were attracted by the magic stone, it was monks who first built on the site in the late 12th century. The building later became the Dower House of the Burgoyne family, who were major landowers in the area. It didn't become a pub officially until 1477, but for several centuries it would have enjoyed life as a centre of the community - a place where on one side the agricultural workers of the day could come to drink and find employment, and on the other the gentry would gather.

The house has also featured in several important novels over the years, and there is a passage in Charles Kingsley's "Westward Ho!" which tells the story of the legendary white bird which has pestered the Oxenham family over the years.

One of the Oxenham ancestors, sailing with Drake's fleet, made the mistake of purloining some live chickens (white ones) from some unfortunate islanders on one of his voyages. Having set sail, his crew plucked the chickens and threw the feathers overboard. A cunning Spanish captain followed the trail of feathers, found the ship, and blew it out of the water. Mr. Oxenham, sadly, was no more, and ever since then the death of a member of the Oxenham family is presaged by the appearence of a mysterious white bird.

On a brighter note, there was a memorable weekend at the pub in the last century when the Rev. Sabine Baring-Gould and Sir Arthur Sullivan invited all the local musicians from miles around to gather and play their songs. These were duly written into a unique record of English folksong. It must have been quite a party and, in a way, lives on in the form of the annual Dartmoor Folk Festival which is held in South Zeal.

Real Ales: Princetown IPA, Princetown Jail.

PETER TAVY INN

Peter Tavy

Off the A386 about three miles north of Tavistock.

Until a few years ago this pub remained almost exactly has it had been when it was built 500 years ago. It has now been refurbished, but one small bar remains, complete with its old beams and flagstone floor. It maintains a link with the past whilst the pub of today offers the customer more up-to-date facilities.

The pub is another of those buildings originally put up for the chaps working on the church, although it did go through a period when the rector was very anti-drinking and would stomp angrily down the lane from the church to berate his parishioners. They, of course, saw him coming and would flee in all directions, leaving their half-drunk pints behind. Such was the power of the church over the lives of ordinary mortals.

Although this was once important mining country, Peter Tavy has always made its living from agriculture. Labourers would tramp to and from their work through the Peter Tavy Coombe and over Cox Tor, placing large pieces of quartz along the side of the path so that they could find their way in the dark. The quartz markers can still be seen, although nowadays you would be well advised to carry a torch as well.

Also on the moorland nearby is a granite post marking the site of Steven's Grave. Steven was an unfortunate young man who fell in love with a local girl. When the parents disapproved of the relationship, he arranged to commit suicide after poisoning the girl, on the grounds that if he could not have her, then no one else could either. Steven went ahead with his side of the arrangement, unaware that the girl had failed to the take the poison, and the poor chap was buried at the local crossroads - gone, but not forgotten.

At some stage in its long life the pub was a useful halt for coaches, with a conveniently placed blacksmith just opposite. Then they moved the main road and Peter Tavy returned to a life of peace and quiet. It did go through a short period of notoriety when it was the haunt of the "Mad Axeman", a Dartmoor prisoner who had got things so well organised that he was allowed out every now and then for a quick pint. One day he never returned and has not been seen since, having, it's thought, met a sticky end somewhere. If nothing else, he'd known a good pub when he found one.

Real Ales: Jail Ale, Bass, guest ales.

TALES FROM THE SNUG

In times past, farm workers in the West Country looked on cider as part of their wages. Most farms had their own cider press and workers would be given up to a couple of gallons a day to help them through their labours. This tradition began when wages were very low, but even when pay improved the cider ration was considered to be a vital aspect of life on the farm, and one of the rights of the labourer.

THE ROYAL INN

Horsebridge

You'll need a good map for this one, but as a starting point, go to Gunnislake and aim north west.

There are those on both sides of the Tamar who believe that Isambard Kingdom Brunel was a bit of a villain for building a bridge joining Devon and Cornwall. Until then in the south of the counties they enjoyed a splendid isolation, broken only by the occasional ferryman across the river. However, Brunel wasn't the first to decide to join the two counties. Back in 1437 a bridge had been built across the Tamar not far from Tavistock, at a point which became known as Horsebridge.

There was already a nunnery on the site and, in those days, most church institutions had a lucrative side-line in providing hospitality, and ale, for passing travellers. The Horsebridge nunnery would have been a useful watering hole for those on their way to and from Cornwall. About a hundred years later, Henry VIII conducted his vendetta against all such establishments, and the Horsebridge nunnery was transformed into an ale house called the Packhorse.

For many years it enjoyed a prime location on what must have been the medieval equivalent of a motorway. It's hard to imagine that today, as the pub now seems hidden away down narrow country lanes, far from the hustle and bustle of passing traffic. It's not easy to find, and it's made even harder by a recent craze for stealing signposts, but it is certainly worth the effort.

For another hundred years it remained the Packhorse. Then Charles I came riding by. I think I would have liked him, as it seems he was forever touring the country and popping into the local for a quick sharpener. There are countless pubs today boasting a one-time visit by the tippling monarch. You can imagine the scene the following day when the landlord told his locals:
"You'll never guess who we had in last night…"
"Oh, yeah!"
In the case of this pub, he could prove it, as the King had ordered the Royal Blacksmith to stamp the Royal Seal into the doorstep, where it can still be seen, although it's looking a bit well-worn by now.

After the King's visit the Packhorse was re-named The Royal, which it remains to this day. No other royal visitors have been recorded, but it's claimed that Turner, the great British painter, stayed there once, sleeping by the big open fire in order to be up in time to paint the bridge at dawn. (There is at least one other pub in the country which claims the same thing!)

Beer lovers should make a special pilgrimage to this place as it is one of the few pubs which brew their own beer on the premises. In days past, nearly all pubs did this, but the practice died out with the expansion of the major breweries. Happily the wheel is turning full circle, and an ever-increasing number of pubs throughout the country are reverting to the joys of their own micro-brewery.

The Royal started brewing again in 1982 and, although the pub changed hands a few years ago, the present landlord wisely decided to keep the brewery. It produces three excellent beers which are only available in the pub, although they do occasionally venture out to beer festivals, and they've picked up a few prizes along the way.

Real Ales: House's own ale, Bass, Sharp's Doom Bar.

TALES FROM THE SNUG

During the 12th century ale was probably an unappetising muddy colour. With no preservatives available it had to be drunk quickly, often before fermentation was complete. In 1497 Leicester brewers were advised to leave their ale for at least an hour before it was sold!

ROYAL OAK

Meavy

Signposted from Yelverton on the A386.

Drinking is a civic duty. Every time you sup a pint of beer you are giving some of your hard-earned money to that nice man, the Chancellor of the Exchequer, who will no doubt spend it on something which you will be thoroughly grateful for.

In the village of Meavy they go one better. Not only does the sizeable price of a pint go to the Exchequer, but another few pence goes to support the village. The pub is owned by the Parish Council and, personally, I cannot think of a better way to pay the rates. It was given to the Parish Council in 1840 on condition that the main room would always be available to the council. The story goes that a few years ago the Parish Coucil actually got rid of one landlord, because he'd made the place too popular with visitors, and locals had to wait too long for a drink.

The building began life as a church house, providing a resting place for monks as they made their way across the moor from Buckfast Abbey to Buckland Abbey. Then along came Charles II who, if all the claims are true, must have spent the best part of two years living in oak trees. It does seem that any pub throughout the land which has an oak tree nearby claims that Charles was up it, giving them an excuse to change the name to The Royal Oak. That is also the claim in Meavy, and whether or not it's true, the oak tree on the green is a magnificent specimen. Estimates of its age range from 800 to 1000 years.

As well as locals, the Royal Oak is a popular watering hole with Plymouthians out for a day in the country. The records show that back in the 16th century, one man was sent to Meavy by Plymouth Corporation. In those days the water in Plymouth was undrinkable, but the Corporation spy discovered that out on the moor it was pure and sweet. His visit led to Sir Francis Drake building his leat which brought fresh water into the City. Meavyians see this as theft, and the only consolation is that the 'spy' was charged two shillings and sixpence for his visit to the pub. An exhorbitant sum in those days.

Today the pub has one smart bar and one drinkers' bar, uncluttered with carpets and tablecloths, where the locals tend to gather to take on board beer rather than food.

Real Ales: Bass, Courage Best.

PERMITTED ACCE

RUGGLESTONE INN

Widecombe

Take the unclassified road out of the village, past the church.

Once this was a deep, uninhabited combe filled only with withy trees. Monks knew about the place as they walked across the moor between abbeys and marked the safe route by stone crosses. During the Middle Ages the miners moved into the relative shelter of the valley, and Withycombe gradually increased in size.

It is alleged that the Devil himself paid a visit to the village. This happened in 1638, when he is also supposed to have popped into the pub at Poundsgate. Perhaps the beer was off, as he was in a foul mood when he reached Widecombe, and he set about attacking the church tower which fell on the congregation below, injuring many of them. History doesn't record what the Devil did next, but there are those who believe that the introduction of excise duty on beer was the work of the Devil, and in 1643, just five years after he wreaked havoc on Dartmoor, a tax on ale was introduced by Parliament. Of course it could just be a coincidence.

Apart from that, nothing much happened in the valley for hundreds of years and Widecombe would have remained happily off the beaten track today but for the Rev. Sabine Baring-Gould. He wrote down the words of an old song which had been sung in the area, recounting the drunken trip across the moor of a few farmers led by one Uncle Tom Cobley. For some reason the song became very popular, and tourists began to arrive in the village to find out more. Widecombe has never looked back, and the Uncle Tom Cobley story has become a major source of income.

While the tourists tend to congregate in and around the centre, most of them miss a wonderful old Dartmoor pub, a few hundred yards out of the village. The Rugglestone Inn is the sort of place of which old Cobley would have approved, and, if he existed at all, it's probable that he would have spent many happy times in the original pub which was just a bit further up the hill. That one burnt down 150 years ago amid stories that it had been deliberately set on fire by angry wives who feared their husbands spent too much time in the place or, alternatively by managers at the local quarry who felt it was affecting the efficiency of their workforce. Whichever story is true, it didn't make a lot of difference as the drinkers simply moved down the road to the new Rugglestone Inn.

Until the early nineties, the pub had no bar and served only beer, cider and wine. The present landlord, Lorrie Ensor, has put in a small bar and now serves spirits as well, but the character of the place has remained firmly planted in the last century. No frills, no fancy decorations, just a tiny bar with a flag-stone floor, a welcoming fire, a great bunch of regulars and the sort of atmosphere which encourages a good chat and some inevitable laughs. The spirit of Cobley lives on, and several of the locals have played the role in the annual Widecombe Fair.

The Rugglestone of the pub's name is a massive lump of granite on the nearby moor. Twenty-two feet long and sixteen feet wide, it's believed to weigh 115 tons. Legend has it that it can only be set in motion with the aid of the church key, but I know of nobody who has tried.

Real Ales: Dartmoor Best, Butcombe.

TAVISTOCK INN

Poundsgate

Half way between Dartmeet and Ashburton.

Walking is one of those activities which I can take or leave (preferably the latter), but if the walk involves a visit to a pub, it suddenly becomes a more attractive proposition, and that is why I have found myself in the Tavistock Inn on several occasions.

It's a pub much frequented by those hardy enthusiasts of the outdoor life - hikers, riders, canoeists, etc. anxious for a good feed, a few pints, and a warm fireside in front of which to defrost and dry out after the Dartmoor mists.

The Devil is not known for his outdoor hobbies, tending to favour a hotter environment, but he apparently called in at The Tavistock while on his way to Widecombe Fair in 1638 (see Rugglestone Inn). One story claims that he paid for his drink with gold coins which turned to shrivelled leaves the moment he left. Another yarn suggests that his pint started to sizzle and boil and left scorch marks on the bar, which is a bit unlikely as bars weren't even introduced to pubs until early in the last century, but never let the facts get in the way of a good story.

Not surprisingly, the pub makes the most of the Devil's visit with a poem to mark the occasion:

He was served with a drink
by the innkeeper's wife
Who, sniffing the brimstone,
went in fear of her life.
The pure golden ale hissed in
his throat
As sparks from his beard lit
him up like the 'tote'.

The glass when returned was
almost red hot;
It burned the old counter —
you can still see the spot.
But thanks to the beer that
the Devil partook
It was too good for evil, so he
slung his hook.

The Tavistock Inn was on one of the main coaching routes across the moor, and many parts of the original coaching inn remain. It's recently been refurbished, but in such a way as to retain the character of the building. Originally it would have been divided into two sections, one for the gentry and one for the not so gentrified. The dividing wall has gone but it still feels like two separate drinking areas with a red-painted 'snug' at the end of the bar.

It's a pleasant pub on a warm summer day but I think it's even better when shrouded in Dartmoor mist with a roaring fire to sit beside.

REAL ALES: Ushers Best, Founders.

THREE CROWNS

Chagford

Opposite the church.

Dartmoor is good pub hunting territory. It may seem remote and bleak to some people, but hiding in the villages and valleys are some wonderful watering holes. The market town of Chagford is particularly well served with pubs.

When historians write about the Civil War, they tend to overlook one fact which I think is rather important. It was Oliver Cromwell who put a tax on beer to help pay for the fight. Kings and governments had tried a similar sort of thing before - need to send another army overseas? Easy, slap a tax on beer, the poor sots will never notice. When Cromwell did it, it stuck, to such an extent that nowadays for every pint we drink, thirty-two pence goes straight into the government's pocket. Never let it be said that we beer drinkers are not doing our bit for the country.

I like to think that young Sydney Godolfin had a premonition of exactly what Cromwell was up to. Sydney was a dashing young cavalier who took on the Roundheads in a skirmish, just outside Chagford. Poor old Sydney was shot in the leg, but he somehow managed to stagger back to the porch of the Three Crowns pub. It was here that Sydney died, but his ghost lingers on inside.

There's said to be another ghost here, that of a lovely young Dartmoor girl called Mary Whyddon, a relative of the man who built the inn. Mary was shot and killed by a jealous lover as she emerged from the church on her wedding day. At the time of her murder, her wedding feast was being prepared in the Three Crowns, and Mary's remains still lie in the church, while her spirit haunts the pub.

All this talk of ghosts might convey the impression that the Three Crowns is a gloomy place. Far from it. It is a magnificent old solid Dartmoor building built in the time of James I, by one John Whyddon, a local lawyer who went to London to seek his fortune and became a judge of the King's Bench. The pub is just off the main square in Chagford, a town which still bustles even though its heyday is long past.

Live music is a regular feature and, on the night I went, there was an enthusiastic trio made up of local roadworkers and refuse men playing an assortment of accordions and a strange instrument made out of beer bottle tops.

So many towns now have only one pub where, on occasions, the landlord gets complacent. With no competition it's too easy not to care about local trade, but in Chagford there's healthy competition between the pubs which is no bad thing for the customers.

Real Ales: Bass, Flowers.

WARREN HOUSE

Postbridge

In the middle of nowhere on the B3212 between Postbridge and Moretonhampstead.

Most pubs are surrounded by sufficient chimney pots to provide a steady local trade, but this one is miles from anywhere high up on Dartmoor. It's almost as remote as it's possible to be in the South West, but it's worth the visit. The Warren House Inn, (its nearest village is Postbridge) is also one of the highest pubs in Britain, beaten only by one in the Yorkshire Dales and another in the Lake District. It's beyond the reach of such modern inventions as electricity so there's the steady hum of a generator providing a warm glow in the old building.

Considering the lack of locals it's remarkable how busy the place is, but there are always a few tourists and travellers in search of a refuge from the wilds of the moor. Many come just to see the fire which, according to the story, has remained alight since the 1840s. The story goes on to say that it was first lit from the burning embers of the original pub, a 14th century ale-house called the New Inn, which was just across the road until it burnt down one night in 1845.

This part of the moor is deserted today, but it was once a thriving tin mining area. Being so far from the nearest supermarket, the men who worked at the Vitifer Mines had to produce their own food, and they turned to rabbits. A full-time warrener was employed to make sure that the rabbits bred (not the most difficult job in the world). The sign above the old inn used to say:

"John Roberts lives here
Sells brandy and beer
Your spirits to cheer;
And should you want meat
To make up the treat,
There be rabbits to eat."

So important were rabbits that the miners even incorporated them into the mine's official seal; three rabbits chasing each other in a circle, a sign which can still be seen on the Warren House Inn. The pub remains true to tradition and rabbit, that most under-rated of cheap foods, regularly appears on the menu. There is also a good selection of ales.

Surprisingly for a pub which doesn't appear to have any nearby 'locals', it still manages to run a darts teams and a pool team, which is a tribute to the landlord's ability to attract people out into the wilds.

Real Ales: Butcombe, Badger Tanglefoot, guest ales.

TALES FROM THE SNUG

It is only recently that water has been taken for granted as a safe drink. Before that it was downright dangerous, as most sources of water were heavily polluted. In the 15th century, Sir John Fortescue wrote that the English peasantry "drink no water unless it be… for devotion." It was reported that Plymouth in 1580 "has for the most part of the year none or at least very little fresh water within a mile of the said town."

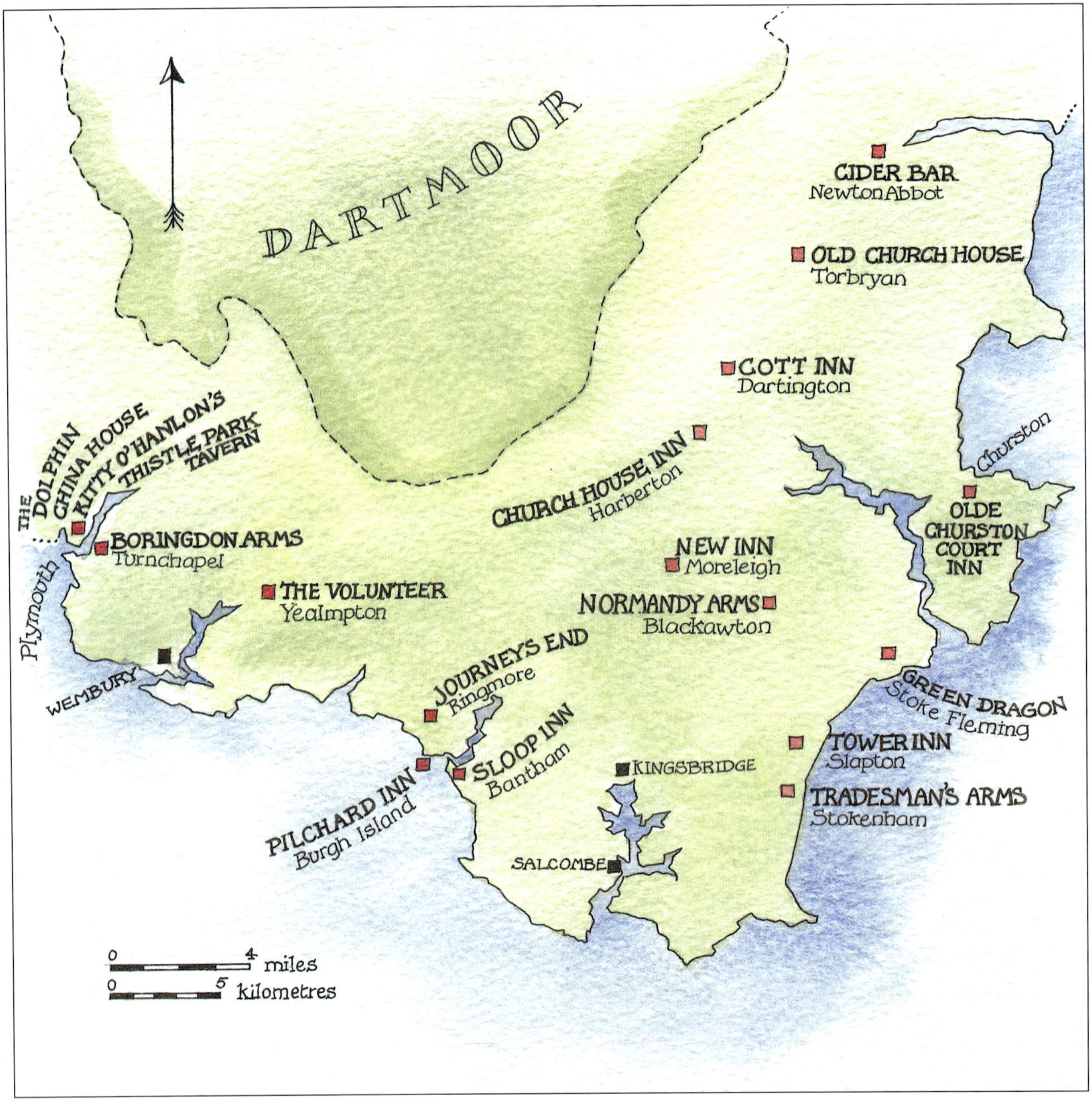
DARTMOOR
CIDER BAR
Newton Abbot
OLD CHURCH HOUSE
Torbryan
COTT INN
Dartington
CHURCH HOUSE INN
Harberton
NEW INN
Moreleigh
NORMANDY ARMS
Blackawton
Churston
OLDE CHURSTON COURT INN
GREEN DRAGON
Stoke Fleming
TOWER INN
Slapton
TRADESMAN'S ARMS
Stokenham
KINGSBRIDGE
SALCOMBE
SLOOP INN
Bantham
PILCHARD INN
Burgh Island
JOURNEYS END
Ringmore
THE VOLUNTEER
Yealmpton
BORINGDON ARMS
Turnchapel
THE DOLPHIN
CHINA HOUSE
KITTY O'HANLON'S
THISTLE PARK TAVERN
Plymouth
WEMBURY
0 4 miles
0 5 kilometres

South Devon

BORINGDON ARMS

Turnchapel

Signposted from the A379 in Plymstock.

Turnchapel has managed to retain its village character despite the fact that over the years Plymouth housing and development has crept ever closer. The new development at Mountbatten has also meant a new influx of people and traffic to the area, but the main village street at Turnchapel remains unspoilt. It's here that you will find the unpretentious terrace building which is the Boringdon Arms. It doesn't look much from the outside but pubs, like books, can't be judged by the cover. Inside, it is refreshingly free of pseudo-pub clutter, and efforts are being made to return the pub to how it must have been a hundred years ago. The carpet has been removed to reveal flagstone floors, and old fireplaces have reappeared.

In the 18th century the building which is now the pub was home to the Quarry Master in charge of the small limestone quarry, the remains of which can be seen at the back of the beer garden. The earliest reference to it becoming a pub is in 1771 when it was bought as an Ale House, and a few years later the Langmead and Co Brewery are on record as having paid £21 7s 6d for a four year lease. Prices may have gone up a fraction since then.

The emphasis at The Bori is on the beer and, as such, it is a local Mecca for ale-hunters. There are normally at least six real ales on offer and twice a month the pub holds a beer festival when the range is enough to satisfy any palate. Not suprisingly, the local branch of CAMRA meets here regularly for enjoyable debate on the merits of the ales.

Turnchapel used to be a major ship-building centre, but gradually the industry moved across the water to Devonport where there was considerably more room, and Turnchapel turned its attention to the leisure side of the boating market.

Up until the fifties there was a regular ferry to and from Plymouth's Barbican. At that time there were three pubs in Turnchapel. The Shipwrights was the locals' pub; the New Inn was used by RAF men from Mountbatten base, and the Bori was where the 'ladies' leant out of the windows facing the ferry to attract their particular type of customers. The ferry has recently been reinstated, but the 'ladies' have left, or so I am told!

One of the largest marinas on the south coast has now opened at Turnchapel and the future of the village seems assured, which must also be good news for the pubs. It's not just a place for yachties though, as the area around Mountbatten has now been incorporated into the South West Coastal Footpath, and attracts the walker-drinkers.

Regular Real Ales: Butcombe, Pitchfork, Summerskills. Always some guest ales.

CHINA HOUSE

Plymouth

By the new Plymouth fish market, Sutton Harbour.

I have a theory that the vast majority of new pubs are designed by a room-full of art college graduates whose sole experience of drinking has been in the Students' Union bar. The aim seems to be to dispense, rather than serve, the beer from long, functional counters which, while making life easier for the bar staff, have about as much charm as the wet fish counter at the local supermarket. A few concessions are made to what we are conditioned to believe is the 'traditional' look, i.e. false oak beams, a handful of so-called Victorian prints of old England, and a few yards of horse brasses. But, other than that, the message the customer generally receives is, "give us your money, get it down you and move on."

The China House is a new pub which breaks that general rule. It has actually been designed with some care to preserve the character of the original building. And the customers are made to feel welcome.

The pub is on the site of a warehouse built back in 1650 by a Plymouth merchant named Rattenbury. It was bought by the Duchy of Cornwall and in 1667 the Commissioners of Victualling used it as a naval storehouse. The great ships of the day would have moored alongside and stocked up with food and ale before setting off on voyages of discovery and warfare. The Marrowbone Slip, right next to the pub, was named after the bones which were thrown out when the beef was boned and put into casks for storage.

During the early part of the 18th century the building had a varied life, being used as a 'King's Bakehouse' a seamen's hospital, a holding shed for prisoners of war and a wool warehouse. Then in 1768 William Cookworthy used the building to produce his famous Plymouth porcelain made from china clay. It was the first time hard-paste porcelain had been produced in Britain, and Mr. Cookworthy employed around sixty people in his factory on the site. That's when it became known as the China House. The porcelain business didn't last long before being moved on to Bristol, and later Staffordshire, but the building found new lives as a timber store, a shipbuilding yard and even a car repair workshop.

In 1989 the brewers came along and converted it into a pub, retaining the warehouse feel in the re-design and utilising all manner of artifacts to give the impression that all they have really done is build a bar in the original building. They have done it with style, and constructed numerous nooks, crannies and waterside decks.

It is a pub with two personalities. At lunchtime it tends to be used by businessmen while in the evening, encouraged by a variety of live music, it becomes more of a students' pub.

Perhaps the China House's greatest asset is Michelle who, at the time of writing, holds the prestigious title National Barmaid of the Year and rightly so, as I know of none better. Among her prodigious talents is the ability to remember the names, along with a few personal details, of more than 800 of her customers, even those who only pop in for a drink once a year. But more than that, she is always there with a smile and a welcome, unlike so many in her chosen profession who seem to think they are doing the customers a real favour just by being behind the bar.

Real Ales: Dartmoor, Marstons Pedigree.

CHURCH HOUSE

Harberton

Signposted off the A381, south west of Totnes.

The monks of years gone by left a wonderful legacy to the pub hunters of today, especially in the South Hams of Devon. Nine hundred years ago they built a chapel in the village of Harberton where they could sing Mass. Today that same room is still in use, but now the Harbertonians sing in praise of the food and drink on offer in what is now called the Church House Inn. Well, they don't actually sing very often, but they are pretty enthusiastic about the place, as are visitors who happen to stumble across the pub.

The big open bar is a room stuffed full of history. There are two latticed windows of hand-made glass on the back wall believed to be the oldest non-ecclesiastical glass panelling in the country, and there is an old oak screen in the corridor which is acclaimed as one of the oldest and finest in existence. The walls are covered with medieval oak panelling and the furniture is a mixture of two or three hundred year old pews and settles. Added to this is a collection of interesting antiques and artefacts, which all contribute to the illusion that you have been transported to a different age.

In 1327 the monks handed what was a Chantry House over to the poor of the area, who no doubt also benefited from the ale brewed on site. Gradually the place became established as an ale and cider house, supplying the needs of the local population. Until the early twentieth century cider remained the main tipple here. It was sold for twopence ha'penny a quart… they didn't bother with pints in those days when men were men, and there was no such thing as a pub-related government health warning.

For those in search of solid sustenance, the Church House offers an interesting selection of specials which are a lot more adventurous than the usual pub fare, and there is also the occasional foodie theme night. While the diners are at one end of the bar, the drinkers at the other have also got a fine selction from which to chose.

Real Ales: Bass, Courage Best and guest ales. Also Churchward's Cider.

TALES FROM THE SNUG

Pub sports involving animals used to be blood thirsty affairs and bear-baiting, cock-fighting and ratting were regular events, designed to pull in the customers. Most of these so called sports have mercifully vanished, although cock-fighting and dog-fighting is still said to take place in some remote pubs. One pub in Durham recently had to abandon a mouse race when it was discovered that fifteen of the eighteen runners were pregnant. In Dorset pub billiard tables were put to use as tracks for tortoise racing, but this sport had to be abandoned in 1938 when a local clergyman complained.

CIDER BAR

Newton Abbot

99 East Street, Newton Abbot.

Once upon a time there were more cider bars than ale houses in the south west, but times and tastes change and now they are rarer than coots with a fine head of hair. You can still buy cider in most places of course, but it is generally the mass-produced, homogenised, pasteurised, bubble-ised stuff that is on offer. Finding proper farmhouse cider is not so easy.

In an end-of-the-terrace building in Newton Abbott the West Country tradition lives on. The Cider Bar is the sort of place you may not even notice as you drive past, but step inside and you will encounter a taste of how things used to be.

Originally this place was a small farmhouse and the part where people stand drinking today was a cobbled track along which locals would travel to market, stopping off to tether their animals and quaff a glass or two of the home brew on their way. It didn't become a licensed cider bar until the early 1900s and it doesn't appear to have changed much since then. Cider was originally served direct from the huge hogshead barrels and, although the bar has changed positions, the place remains true to the original.

Real Devon cider is still served straight from the barrel. It is of varying strengths and flavours, all of which are guaranteed to go straight to the legs. That's the trouble with cider. It is so drinkable that the brain is fooled into believing it's an innocuous little beverage. The legs know otherwise, but refuse to tell you until the time comes to stand up. They then tend to travel in opposing directions, leaving the torso no alternative but to collapse onto the floor, much to the merriment of seasoned, better trained imbibers.

If you turn up here on a Sunday lunchtime you will witness a strange ritual which has been going on since the early days of the Bar. The Long Bar Cork Club meets every Sunday lunchtime without fail. It has around forty members, all of whom must carry a cork encased in a small metal tube. During the week they meticulously record in a ledger the misdemeanours of fellow members... such heinous crimes as failing to buy a round, spilling someone's drink or insulting someone's girlfriend. At the Sunday lunchtime session the members are tried for their crimes and invariably a fine of a few pence is imposed. The most serious offence seems to be being caught without your cork.

Over twelve months all these fines add up to a sizeable kitty (as much as £3000 in a good year) which the members then spend on an annual outing. Needless to say the outing also involves just a drop or two of apple loopy juice.

Cider bars might possibly conjure up images of dark holes full of sinister characters with purple noses. I even know one or two hardened beer drinkers who are frightened to go into such places. Forget the image. This Cider Bar in Newton Abbot is a real family watering hole with a good friendly atmosphere.

Real Ales: Don't even ask for one.

TALES FROM THE SNUG

Thomas Westcote in his view of Devon in 1630 praised cider "a drink both pleasant and healthy, much desired of seamen for long southern voyages".

Cott Inn
Licensed Since 1320AD
Luncheon

COTT INN

Dartington

Signposted off the A385, 2 miles north of Totnes.

No book about West Country pubs is really complete without the Cott Inn, which is reputedly one of the oldest pubs in the country.

Today the emphasis in the pub is very much on food and wine. It was named Wine Pub of the Year in 1996, but it wasn't always so. The Cott first became a pub during the reign of Edward II in 1320. In those days, one of the most important forms of transport was the humble old mule, and the pub was set up on the mule track between Totnes and Ashburton. The top end of the building was used for providing shelter and fodder for the animals, while the muleteers, trading mainly in wool and animal hides, refreshed themselves next door.

The most successful of these early traders was, apparently, a Dutchman, although nobody is sure how he ended up in deepest Devon at a time when international travel was not exactly easy. His name was Johannes Cott, and he was so successful they named the pub and surrounding hamlet after him.

Dartington is an unusual village in that it is bisected by main roads with a busy roundabout at its centre, and yet it is a thriving community, thanks largely to the Elmhirst family who arrived here in 1925. They breathed new life into Dartington Hall, founded a new school, and led the way for new business to spring up in and around the village. Today Dartington has an international reputation as a centre for the arts. Incidentally, there is an interesting little bar in the Hall itself which is worth seeking out.

Many visitors arrive here in search of the home of Dartington Glass, which is a bit of a disappointment as the Glassworks are at the other side of the county, in Torrington. Such visitors are often to be found seeking solace in the Cott.

REAL ALES: Directors, Bass.

TALES FROM THE SNUG

Only a few centuries ago there was no alternative but to drink ale, which was considered a much safer and more enjoyable option than water. Indeed, drinking water carried with it a kind of social stigma. Andrew Boorde, a 16th century social commentator, said "water is not wholesome sole by itself for an Englishman."

THE DOLPHIN

Barbican, Plymouth

Opposite the old fishmarket and new Dartington Glassworks on the Barbican.

The Dolphin is a real pub and one of my favourite watering holes, not least because the quality of the Bass is second to none. Rich sparkling colour, fresh taste, with just the right bitterness, served straight from the barrel. Billy, the landlord, is a true cellarman who knows and cares for his beer. I defy you to find a better pint.

While the beer is fresh, the bar looks and feels as if it has been around for hundreds of years, which, of course, it has. The Pilgrim Fathers last set foot in England on the quay just up the road from The Dolphin, now known as the Mayflower Steps (a badly, and shamefully, neglected monument to the founders of America). I like to think that the Pilgrims enjoyed a last pint of ale in the Dolphin before setting off on their adventure. They were apparently not averse to the odd pint or two, as one story tells how they cut short their voyage along the coast of America in order to put ashore at the first possible landfall in order to brew up fresh supplies of beer. But for that, New England may have ended up in Florida.

The Dolphin has survived all the upheavals in pub fashion which have destroyed so many other old pubs. There has been a bit of restructuring over the years, but it remains a basic boozer with stone floors, simple furniture and a refreshing absence of horse brasses and twee illustrations. What you will find on the walls are some of the works of that wonderful artist Beryl Cook, who has been a regular in the Dolphin for about thirty years. The pub has been the inspiration for many of her paintings, and it's not hard to see why. For Beryl, a good pub has to have one most important feature… "lots of people having a bloody good time!" . The Dolphin has that in bucket loads.

All human life is in The Dolphin and, at any one time, you'll find suited businessmen rubbing shoulders with local fishermen, the occasional gentlemen of the road and heavily jewelled examples of Plymouth's glitterati popping in for a pre-theatre drink.

As for food, forget it. The Dolphin is purely a drinkers' pub but, if you happen to be overcome with a desire for the solid stuff, there are good fish 'n' chip shops nearby, and Billy has no objection to you bringing some back to eat in his pub, provided of course you have a beer or two as well. And you can't ask fairer than that.

Real Ales: Bass.

TALES FROM THE SNUG

For hundreds of years bored drinkers have invented weird and wonderful games to brighten up the occasional dull evening. Some pubs still play Dwile Flonking, which involves two teams hitting each other with long poles and beer-soaked dishcloths. Then, of course, there is Conga Cuddling where a five foot eel is used to knock over human skittles; Rhubarb Thrashing, where the contestants stand in dustbins in order to beat each other with rhubarb; and Dratting, which involves rushing through the pub with a long pole, being careful not to Nurdle.

GREEN DRAGON

Stoke Fleming

A few miles west of Dartmouth on A379.

The coast road between Dartmouth and Kingsbridge is an attractive drive, a fact not unknown to thousands of tourists every year, but there are several good watering holes along the route to ease the tension of heavy traffic.

The Green Dragon at Stoke Fleming is only a hundred yards off the main road, but most visitors to the area miss this treat.

The exact early history of the place is vague, but there are records of a building on the site dating back to 1170 when it was more than likely to have been connected with the building of the church opposite. It has been a pub since the mid-seventeenth century and remains basic and simple, with good beer and good food. There is a regularly changing menu making the most of all local ingredients.

Peter and Alix Crowther have run the pub since 1993. Peter is a well-known single-handed yachtsman who for over twenty years had a memorable partnership with his junk-rigged yacht, Galway Blazer. Sadly the yacht hit something solid during a transatlantic race and sank, but there are many photographs, paintings and models of her around the bar. The solitary life of a single-handed sailor would seem to be at odds with the gregarious life of a pub landlord, but somehow Peter combines the two. No doubt he relishes the peace and quiet of a long sea voyage after a busy season in the Green Dragon.

Over the centuries the sea has obviously been a strong influence on the pub which, like so many coastal pubs, boasts secret smugglers tunnels nearby, through which illicit booze was brought in away from the inquisitive eye of the revenue men. In a lot of cases these smugglers tunnels turn out to be figments of beer-fuelled imaginations, but not in Stoke Fleming. At least one of the tunnels near the Green Dragon still exists, but I have been sworn to secrecy about its exact location. After all, the customs men are still not too happy about cheap booze being smuggled in from the Continent.

Real Ales: Flowers IPA, Royal Oak, Wadworths 6X.

JOURNEYS END

Ringmore

Signposted from B3392 road to Bigbury.

The picture postcard South Devon village of Ringmore seems a most unlikely location in which to write a drama of tragedy, death and destruction, but it was here that the author R.C. Sheriff wrote his famous play "Journeys End", set in the trenches of World War One. The pub adopted the name of the play, but today the only signs of fighting are in the well battered face of the pub cat, Tigger, a bruiser if ever I saw one.

The history of the pub dates back way before the First World War. It was originally built in 1190 as a cottage to house the builders who built the church. They quarried the stones for the church from what is now the car park just up the road. About a hundred years later, in 1290, it became a simple cider and ale house and remained as such until the time of Elizabeth I. She decided in her wisdom that there should be drinking houses to support the coaches as they travelled across the country, and she opened a chain of New Inns. The Ringmore pub found itself being upgraded to become a New Inn, although its hard to understand why, as it isn't really on a coaching route to or from anywhere particular. It was a respectable pub though. A church document of 1685 describes it as "a house of good order, no cards, no dice to be used."

She was a drinkers' friend this Queen Elizabeth. As well as setting up new pubs, she also declared that all brewers must make and sell beer within the financial reach of her subjects. She would have greatly disapproved of some of these ridiculously expensive designer beers which the marketing people are foisting on us today.

Another piece of legislation about that time decreed that, if a brewer should fail to produce beer, the equipment would be confiscated and given to someone else who could, thus ensuring that no one ever went short of the daily pint.

The whole area around Ringmore was notorious for smugglers who no doubt spent many happy hours, plotting and drinking in the pub. There is a rumour that a tunnel links the pub to nearby Ayrmer Cove, which is one of those smugglers dream beaches, ideal for landing contraband booty. At one stage the local revenue men, no doubt aware of all this, set up their headquarters in the pub which must have put a bit of a damper on their activities.

Good Queen Bess would, I suspect, have loved the Journey's End, a pub which is justifiably renowned for its regular range of thoroughly good real ales. It also stages Beer Festivals in Spring and Autumn when there are twenty or so beers to chose from.

The basic fabric of the building hasn't changed much over the centuries, although a recent addition is a conservatory. This may not be the prettiest bit of architecture but it's somewhere to hide the noisier kids and dogs!

Real Ale: Otter, Exmoor, and several guest ales.

KITTY O'HANLON'S

Plymouth

St Andrew Street.

The Irish have long held a reputation for knowing how to enjoy themselves, especially when it comes to a glass or two of the loopy juice. Based on this reputation, the last twenty years has seen a sudden appearance in main streets up and down England of a whole string of Irish theme pubs, all looking just the same, all filled with fake Irish road signs, all serving stout and all playing diddly-doo hooligan music.

I ought to hate them, but there is something about Kitty O'Hanlon's which sets it apart from the usual Irish pub. For a start the man behind it, Tom Mooney, is a real Irishman, which helps. It's also a pub with a bit of history.

It may not be the oldest pub in the City, but there has been an establishment selling booze on this site since the days of the Crusades, so it is certainly one of the oldest drinking locations. The original pub was called the Turk's Head and was a classic medieval building. For some reason it was pulled down in the 1860s and replaced with a pub called The Abbey, which suggests that it had some sort of connection with the church. In fact it took its name from the Prysten House nearby.

For many years it was a favourite haunt of all those using the Magistrates Court next door. At one end of the bar would be defendants and their supporters (the defendant would be the one in the suit), the lawyers would stand in a separate area, and in another corner would be the journalists swapping stories of how things used to be… and good stories they were too.

Things haven't changed much since the pub was renamed Kittys in 1994. By day it is still the haunt of users of the Courts, and by night a generation of younger drinkers moves in, making it one of the most popular city centre pubs.

Rumour has it that the pub may be changing hands again, and it is uncertain whether or not the Irish theme will carry on. Whatever happens, the long history of drinking on this site is likely to continue for many years to come.

Real Ales: Bass, (Guinness, of course).

NEW INN

Moreleigh

Signposted off the A381 at Halwell, between Kingsbridge and Totnes.

One of my great pleasures in life is driving along a quiet road through glorious contryside and suddenly coming across an interesting looking pub. That is how it was a few years ago when I first discovered the New Inn, one of the unsung heroes of the pub world which goes on through the centuries, dispensing good ale and food without ever making it into the usual guide books. It is purely and simply a country pub with no frills and no gimmicks, and all the better for it.

Moreleigh appears today as a sleepy little village where nothing much happens, but back in the 13th century when the original pub was built, it was the

TALES FROM THE SNUG

In 1830 the Government introduced a Beer Act which was to revolutionise drinking throughout the land. For three hundred years there had been fairly tight legislation on pubs and ale houses, but this Act came as an antidote. It allowed virtually any householder to sell beer provided he or she obtained an excise permit. In the same year, excise duties on beer were repealed. It was partly hoped to revive beer sales which had flagged because of competition from spirit sellers. It was also a way for the Tory prime minister, Wellington, to regain popular support. In the first year after the Beer Act, 24,000 new beer houses opened.

centre of a wealthy agricultural area. Farmers brought their animals to Moreleigh for the big market which was once held in the village, and no doubt in those days the New Inn was one of many ale-houses providing much needed refreshment. The market disappeared when Moreleigh was all but wiped out by the Great Plague.

During the 1600s the pub was 'modernised', and became the main courthouse for the Stanborough Hundreds, an area which stretched from Kingsbridge to Buckfastleigh. The old steps up the the high-ceilinged courtroom can still be seen at the front of the pub. It was also the place where the good men and true of the area who were appointed constables, came to collect their pay and to report the misdemeanours of the populace. While the business of law went on upstairs, the pub carried on its activities below.

Since that modernisation there has been very litle change to the New Inn. There is still just the one bar area with beer served straight from the barrel.

Real Ale: Palmers.

NORMANDY ARMS

Blackawton

South of the A3122 between Halwell and Dartmouth.

Blackawton is a peaceful little village in the middle of the lovely South Hams countryside. For centuries people have decided this is a pretty good area to set up home as the village dates back to Saxon times and there's been a church here since the Normans.

This part of the coast around Slapton bears a remarkable similarity to the beaches of Normandy, a fact which led to it being used during the last war as a practice area for the D-Day landings. It was a tragic time, as testified by the war memorial on the beach, listing the American GIs who died here. The village of Blackawton was at the centre of things during this period, when all the inhabitants of this

and other villages in the area were evacuated to make way for the troop movements. In the Normandy Arms there is still much talk and speculation as to what exactly went on when the villagers left.

One bar of The Normandy Arms is like a living museum to that strange episode during the war. A contemporary notice on the wall gives details of the mass evacuation of the area when, in 1943, six thousand people were suddenly told to leave their homes. You can imagine what the conversation was like in the pub in those days. These were people who had lived for generations in the area and had probably rarely been further than nearby Totnes. Now they were being forced from their homes, and a large part of the South Hams was effectively sealed off as the GIs underwent their training.

For some reason the American forces used live ammunition during this training, a fact which led to many deaths. However, the worst incident came when German torpedo boats attacked landing craft as they manoeuvred in a training exercise off the coast. Seven hundred men died. The conversation in the Normandy and other pubs in the area still frequently returns to the events of the War, and there are persistent rumours that the bodies of many of the victims are buried in the fields around Blackawton.

Blackawton used to have its own brewery but, although the name carries on, the brewery has moved a couple of miles away to the village of Washbourne.

Real Ales: Blackawton, Devon Gold.

TALES FROM THE SNUG

A barmaid, Elinour Rumming, who kept an alehouse in Leatherhead in Henry VIII's reign was described as:

"Droopy and drowsy
Scurvy and lowsy
Her face all bowsy
Comely crinkled
Wondrously wrinkled
Like a roast pig's ear
Bristled with hair".

Things have generally improved since then!

OLD CHURCH HOUSE

Torbryan

Off the A381 to the north west of Ipplepen, signposted.

A good general rule when travelling in a strange area and feeling in need of a drink is to search the horizon for the church tower. As often as not there will be a pub nearby.

Hundreds of old pubs throughout the country began life as cottages built to accommodate the chaps who were working on the building of the church. Most of them were built from materials which were not considered good enough for the church itself, the quarry waste. When the church was finished, these cottages went through a period of being used by the clerics as a place to offer bed, board and beer to other clerics and visiting pilgrims. Gradually over the years many of them developed into ale houses and, ultimately, into the pubs we know today. With remarkable originality, they were called Church House Inns.

There is no shortage of Church House inns in the South Hams of Devon, but there is only one Old Church House and that is in Torbryan, tucked away in a valley between the busy A38 to the north and the tourist tracks to the south. Today, this little village is hidden well off the beaten track, but not so long ago it was an important staging post on the route from Plymouth to Exeter.

In the centre of fertile agricultural land, this was rich countryside, most of which was in the hands of two families, the Gilberts and the Champerknownes, who would alleviate the boredom of long evenings without a television by arranging cock-fighting tournaments in the pub. Thousands of pounds were won and lost.

From earlier times, an old Saxon door is still in place as an outside feature. It is not used now, but it once led into a room which features what is believed to be the largest pub fireplace in the country. This is where travellers of the past would pull up a bit of old sacking and sleep for the night. Some travellers

got better treatment. According to the records, Henry VII called in for the night and thought the pub was so good he later recommended it to his son. Number Eight is also said to have been a visitor. This would have been round about the time he was trying to ban brewing ale with hops which he believed adulterated the flavour, and Henry VIII knew a thing or two about adulterating.

A souvenir of another monarch is a set of Elizabethan bowling pins which hang from the ceiling. When the game was played in her day they used just five pins, but every century an extra one was added until it evolved into today's ten-pin game.

Another feature of the pub is a fine wooden screen at the end of the bar. This dates back to the time of the Armada, when the entrepreneurs of the day made a few pounds by flogging off bits of the shipwrecks to anyone who needed a nice bit of panelling for the front room. Not many people could afford their prices, so the bits of ship-scrap often ended up in the hands of some of the more prosperous pubs of the day. It's believed that the one in the Old Church House began its life as a cross section of a Spanish galleon.

With its long history, it should come as no surprise that the Old Church House is home to a ghost or two. Leaving the spirits aside, the beer is good too.

Real Ales: Marstons, Church House Specials.

TALES FROM THE SNUG

Henry VIII was not exactly known for his prudish views, but during his reign he decided to close down the many 'stews' that were operating throughout the land. These were houses which specialised in 'the oldest profession'. All that happened was that the prostitutes moved into the ale houses instead. In the early 17th century one pub advertised "a pot of ale, a pipe of tobacco and a pocksy whore for 3d."

OLDE CHURSTON COURT INN

Churston

Signposted from the A3022 Brixham Road.

By any standards, the Ye Olde Churston Court Inn is rather grander than the average 'local'. It is an impressive manor house set just back from the busy Cornish Riviera in the comparative peace and quiet of the parish of Churston Ferrers.

Don't be put off by the imposing exterior. The interior is pretty imposing too, but it is a fascinating place to enjoy a meal and a drink or two while immersing yourself in local history. The Manor dates back to 1016 when it was owned by a chap called Ulf. His son Ludhael became a Lord of Totnes, and it was an order of monks from Totnes who used the manor as a monastery for a couple of centuries. One of the monks still uses it today, as he appears frequently in ghostly form in the Armour room.

Another ghost appears to be a chambermaid of the late 1600s, which is round about the time the building became an Inn. She is said to hover about in one of the first floor bedrooms, much to the alarm of the landlord's two English mastiffs (big hairy soft creatures with the names Athelston and Britannia). With all these spirits lurking about the place, it is appropriate that the local group of paranormal investigators has chosen the Churston Court as the venue for its regular meetings.

As you might expect, the building has played host to many famous and infamous guests over the years. Agatha Christie was a regular visitor, and even donated a stained glass window to the church next door. The Great Train Robber, Bruce Reynolds, hid out here for a while, attracting much attention from the local constabulary who searched the place from top to bottom. Too late, the man had fled.

When Peter Malkin took over this old manor house in 1991, the old flagstones had been cemented over, magnificent granite fireplaces were blocked up, and ancient walls hidden behind thick plaster. Fortunately, he is passionate about restoring

medieval buildings, and he spent some years bringing the place back to its former glory. During his work here he has uncovered all manner of interesting objects including musket balls, old coins, clay pipes and even a 16th century suit of armour hidden in a fireplace.

Churston Court is a maze of rooms for diners, drinkers and guests. They range from the old kitchen, which has been converted into a grand manorial dining room, to tiny 'snugs' where a drink can be enjoyed in privacy. Amazingly, considering the ancient splendour of it all, the main bar still manages to retain the feel of a pub, and it is well supported by locals and visitors alike.

One other feature worth mentioning is a Victorian upright piano in one of the rooms. It's not there just for decoration, though. Once a week Pam, a local pianist, comes in for a good old fashioned sing song and knees up. You don't see that too often nowadays.

Real Ales: Dartmoor Best.

PILCHARD INN

Burgh Island

Go to Bigbury-on-Sea, and work it out for yourself, according to the state of the tide!

There are occasions when just getting to the pub is an experience in itself, and I have to abandon my faithful companion, Doris. Getting to the 14th century Pilchard Inn on Burgh Island is one of those occasions, and the pub is definitely worth a visit for those with a fascination for strange forms of transport. The Burgh Island sea tractor is famous, a one-off devised by a combination of local ingenuity, eccentricity and, I suspect, a chap who had had one glass too many. It carries punters from the mainland to the tiny private island off the South Devon coast. Of course, you could just wait for the tide to go out, save yourself fifty pence and walk across, but it's not quite so much fun.

The island was once home to a small religious community, with a monastery on the site of what is now the art deco hotel. On the hill top was the lookout point for the local fishermen. The look-out, or 'Huer', as he was called, would scan the Channel for the tell-tale signs of the pilchard shoals, and as soon as he spotted something he'd cry out (that's where "hue and cry" comes from). The fishermen in the pub would down their pints and put to sea.

The pilchard fleet is long gone, but the memory lives on in the pub. Memories too of the days of smuggling, for this was once the base of the notorious smuggler Tom Crocker. For years he escaped capture until one fateful night when the preventive officers caught up with him and shot him dead right outside the pub. All that remains of Tom now is his effigy which, with a little bit of imagination, you can just about make out at the side of the fireplace at the Pilchard. There used to be a dreadful pub called The Tom Crocker on the mainland opposite Burgh Island, but mercifully it's been demolished.

Unlike so many seaside pubs with their carefully created smugglers bars, and pirates parlours and lavatories marked 'Gulls' and 'Buoys', The Pilchard is the genuine article. Inevitably a pub surrounded by the sea is stuffed full of bits and pieces gathered over the years on rocks and wrecks. Even the ship's parrot is here. Once, Laura (strange name for a parrot) sat in the corner of the bar, occasionally joining in conversations and giving customers a friendly, if painful, nibble. Now, she is a deceased

parrot. She's passed on, allegedly through too much booze in the birdseed, but her cold eyes continue to keep a check on goings-on.

The Pilchard may be only a few hundred yards from the mainland but that short stretch of water enables life there to be lived at a different pace, dictated by the tides. There was a time not so long ago when if high tide here coincided with closing time, the sea tractor would quite remarkably just break down. It was the perfect lock-in. Sadly that sort of thing doesn't happen anymore.

Real Ales: Courage.

SLOOP INN

Bantham

Signposted at the Churchstow roundabout on the A379.

A great many visitors to the South West are afraid to venture too far off the main roads and highways into the narrow lanes and byeways. They are missing some real treats for, as often as not, at the end of the lanes can be found a delightful pub. The lane to Bantham is a good example because just before the road runs into the sea, lies the Sloop Inn.

Bantham is on the banks of the River Avon, an estuary which has remained remarkably unspoilt in such a popular tourist area. There has been a settlement at Bantham since the Iron Age, and recent archaeological discoveries in the area lend weight to the belief that two thousand years ago this was also an important area for tin trading. Despite the difficult conditions at the mouth of the Avon, Bantham was for many years a busy little port, and over the centuries it has seen more than its fair share of continental raiders keen to plunder its riches.

This is fishing and farming country, and the pub began life as a farmhouse back in the 16th century. Then, as now, there was not a lot of money to be made from agriculture, so a penny or two was made on the side by brewing and selling ale. There was a ready market for the stuff from the thirsty fishermen who lived and worked in the village. The fishermen, in turn, no doubt helped to supplement the pub's stocks with a regular supply of smuggled booze, and the Sloop Inn developed into a thriving pub. In the 18th century one of the landlords was a Mr. John Whiddon, who had something of a reputation in the area. A notorious member of the smuggling fraternity, his name also crops up with that of old Uncle Tom Cobley on that famous trip to Widecombe Fair.

The pub used to mint its own coins which were used to make purchases throughout the local community. Kingsbridge Museum has a collection of these coins, and the pub also has a few to show off to interested customers.

Local historian Kendall McDonald, in his excellent book about the area, tells a nice story of how, at the turn of the century, the locals claimed you could tell where a man came from by his trousers. A man with a patch on the seat of his trousers came from Bantham, while Thurlestone men had no patches. The reason for this was that the Sloop Inn had wooden benches for its drinkers, while the Village Inn at Thurlestone had no such luxuries, and the locals had to stand and drink.

While offering a good selection of real ales, the Sloop also has an excellent reputation for its food, particularly fish. The Giant Cod and Chips is a particular favourite for those with a healthy appetite.

Real Ales: Blackawton, Flowers IPA, Bass.

THISTLE PARK TAVERN

Plymouth

Sutton Road, Plymouth.

The Coxside area of Plymouth has undergone a transformation in recent years. This used to be a not particularly attractive working area of the city, with a busy dock and all the industrial paraphernalia that went with it - gasometers, railway lines, warehouses etc. Today, it is rapidly becoming the leisure centre of Plymouth, with the new aquarium, a huge entertainment complex, a marina and new pubs. The fish market has also moved to this side of Sutton Harbour, bringing with it yet more business.

At the centre of Coxside is a wonderful old pub which has carried on unchanged through the good times and the bad.

The Thistle Park Tavern dates back to the early 19th century and the days when there was a large open space in the area, which was full of thistles. Cutting them down, as most proud park keepers would do, would have involved a bit too much effort. It was far easier to let them grow and simply re-name the park.

For the best part of a century the railway line ran within a few feet of the door of the pub, but that has now been replaced by a busy crossroads, so it is not the most peaceful location. Unlike some of the smart new pubs in the area, the Thistle Park remains dedicated to the simple demands of serious beer fanciers who are unimpressed by deep-pile carpets and fancy furniture. The bare floor is polished mahogany, and the seating is made out of old church pews from Launceston Methodist Church. I'm not sure if the staunch Methodists would have approved, but I reckon they are being put to good use.

The other reason beer lovers like the place is that the Thistle Park is a brew pub, the home of Sutton Brewery. This was set up by ex-South African paratrooper, Quinten Style, who originally came to England in search of surfing and rugby. His brewery

TALES FROM THE SNUG

American president, Benjamin Franklin liked his ale. He declared once: "Beer is living proof that God loves us and wants to see us happy."

now reularly supplies about 40 pubs in the area with, amongst other ales, the excellent award-winning XSB.

Quinten, known as 'Biltong' to the regulars, has naturally brought a South African touch to the pub, with one or two of his home dishes on the menu and, when there are a few of his fellow countrymen in the place, the occasional South African sing-song. It all adds up to a lively atmosphere, good company and great beer.

Real Ales: Sutton Brews, and South African beers.

TOWER INN

Slapton

In the village of Slapton, signposted off the A379.

Having been brought up at a time when Robin Hood stories were the big hits of children's television, I have always wondered why Friar Tuck appeared such a jovial old soul. It was many years before I discovered the reason - he was permanently plastered. I now know that the monks of old spent a great deal of time brewing ale and drinking the result. It was such a part of the monastic life that at least one abbey used to provide its residents with two gallons of the stuff every day.

The exact story of what went on at the Collegiate Chantry of St Mary has been lost in the mists of time, but it's a fairly safe bet that the inmates enjoyed the odd tipple.

Today all that remains of this religious organisation, which was set up in 1372 by Edward III's standard bearer, is a derelict tower in the South Devon village of Slapton, next to which is a wonderful little pub called, not surprisingly, The Tower.

The Tower Inn is on the site of the old chantry, and it continues the tradition of merry imbibing, with a justly earned reputation for real ales. During the "Red Barrel Age" when the breweries tried to foist gassy keg beers on the unsuspecting public, the Tower Inn persisted in supplying proper beer to grateful customers, and this was before the days of CAMRA. It remains today what it always has been, a friendly little pub with a welcoming atmosphere to encourage the appreciation of good beer. The atmosphere is sometimes enhanced by music from local talent.

To get to the pub involves manoeuvering through twisting lanes and vary narrow gaps between the cottages, ending up in a tiny car park. Best leave the car outside the village and walk!

A speciality of this area used to be a brew known as "White Ale". It had a reputation throughout the country, and one 19th century writer described it as "the nappiest beer in all England". It was also described as "the wholesomest, whereby many in elder times lived a hudred years."

Some say the ale was introduced to the area by a French doctor looking after French prisoners of war in Kingsbridge Barracks during the 18th century. It was such a common and popular brew that the villagers of Dodbrooke near Kingsbridge used to pay their tithes with white ale. Somehow the recipe for the stuff seems to have been forgotten, which is probably a good thing as I am told that one of the essential ingredients was pigeon droppings.

Real Ales: Tanglefoot, Exmoor, Bishops Tipple and guest ales.

TRADESMAN'S ARMS

Stokenham

In the centre of the village, off the A379.

The South Hams is particularly good pub-hunting territory, and it seems it has been like this for at least 600 years. The Tradesman's Arms is another South Hams pub dating back to the fourteenth century when life in the area may have been tough, but there was no shortage of watering holes.

Stokenham lies about a mile inland from Slapton Sands. In medieval times most coastal settlements were built slightly away from the shore in order to deter raiders, or at least to give the residents warning of raiders arriving by sea. The village was at one stage a Royal farm, given to Anne of Cleves by Henry VIII in one of his more generous moments.

The Tradesman's Arms is one of two good pubs in the village which date back to a time when most such establishments in the area were cider houses. The Tradesman's was different in that it also brewed its own ale, and tradesmen would come from miles around for a taste of something other than fermented apple juice. The old brewhouse can still be seen behind the existing kitchen, and the pub you see today is the result of this building and three old cottages gradually merging into one.

For some reason the pub has spent most of the past 150 years being run by ex-servicemen, but it is now in new, non-Forces, hands. Current landlord John Sharman's background is in catering, and there is a strong emphasis on food in the Tradesman's Arms nowadays. As he is a keen shot and an angler, there is usually a good selection of fish and game, and as John limits meals to 40 covers at a time, everything is freshly and individually cooked. There is space at the bar for those not interested in taking solids.

A surprising number of pubs in the South Hams tend not to stick to the standard lunchtime and evening opening sessions, particularly during the winter. It can lead to the occasional disappointment, as I know to my cost! The Tradesman's Arms, for example, is closed on Saturday lunchtimes, Sunday evenings and all day Monday. Don't ask me why, but it apparently works.

Real Ales: Adnams Broadside, Young's Oatmeal Stout.

TALES FROM THE SNUG

Pubs may have been ideal recruiting grounds for the army and navy, but unfortunately it meant that most recruits were far too fond of the ale to fight properly. The historian William of Malmsebury, writing back in the 12th century, said that one of the reasons the Normans won the Battle of Hastings was because the English army had all been over-doing the loopy juice causing us to attack "more with rashness and precipitate fury than with military skill." The English, he said, were accustomed to "eat till they became surfeited and drink till they were sick". But for that weakness, Harold may never, perhaps, have got one in the eye.

THE VOLUNTEER

Yealmpton

A few miles east of Plymouth, on the A379.

It fronts onto a busy main road. It doesn't have a large convenient car park. There is not a lot to distinguish it from the other buildings in the terrace. Three reasons why most people speed past The Volunteer without a second glance, leaving it to be enjoyed by the locals and those in the know. The "Vollie" is proof, once again, that you can't judge a pub by looking at its cover.

On one side of the front door is a proper drinkers' bar with a pool table, and walls and ceilings covered

with ships' crests. It is just the place for some serious games of spoof, and the regular pub quiz. On the other side, for those who prefer it, is the lounge bar and dining area.

In recent years, the Vollie has gained a much-deserved reputation for the quality of its food. This is not the usual run-of-the-mill pub grub, but an interesting, well-prepared selection of dishes all served in a relaxed, informal manner. The 'fun factor' is an active ingredient of eating and drinking at the Volunteer!

In winter, the pub is all low ceilings, thick walls and roaring fires.

The building obviously goes back a long way, but no-one seems too sure about its history, although in the early nineteenth century there was reference to a pub called the Rifle Volunteer. By 1886 it appears that the Rifle bit was dropped. It is probable that it was another of those pubs which acted as an assembly point for the local men to volunteer, or be 'volunteered', against their will, into the Services. In years past the admirals and generals didn't bother with such refinements as recruiting agencies when they needed a few more fighting men. They knew it was a lot easier to catch the poor chaps down at the pub, and get them to take the King's Shilling *before* they had a chance to sober up.

Real Ales: Bass, Courage Best, Summerskill's.

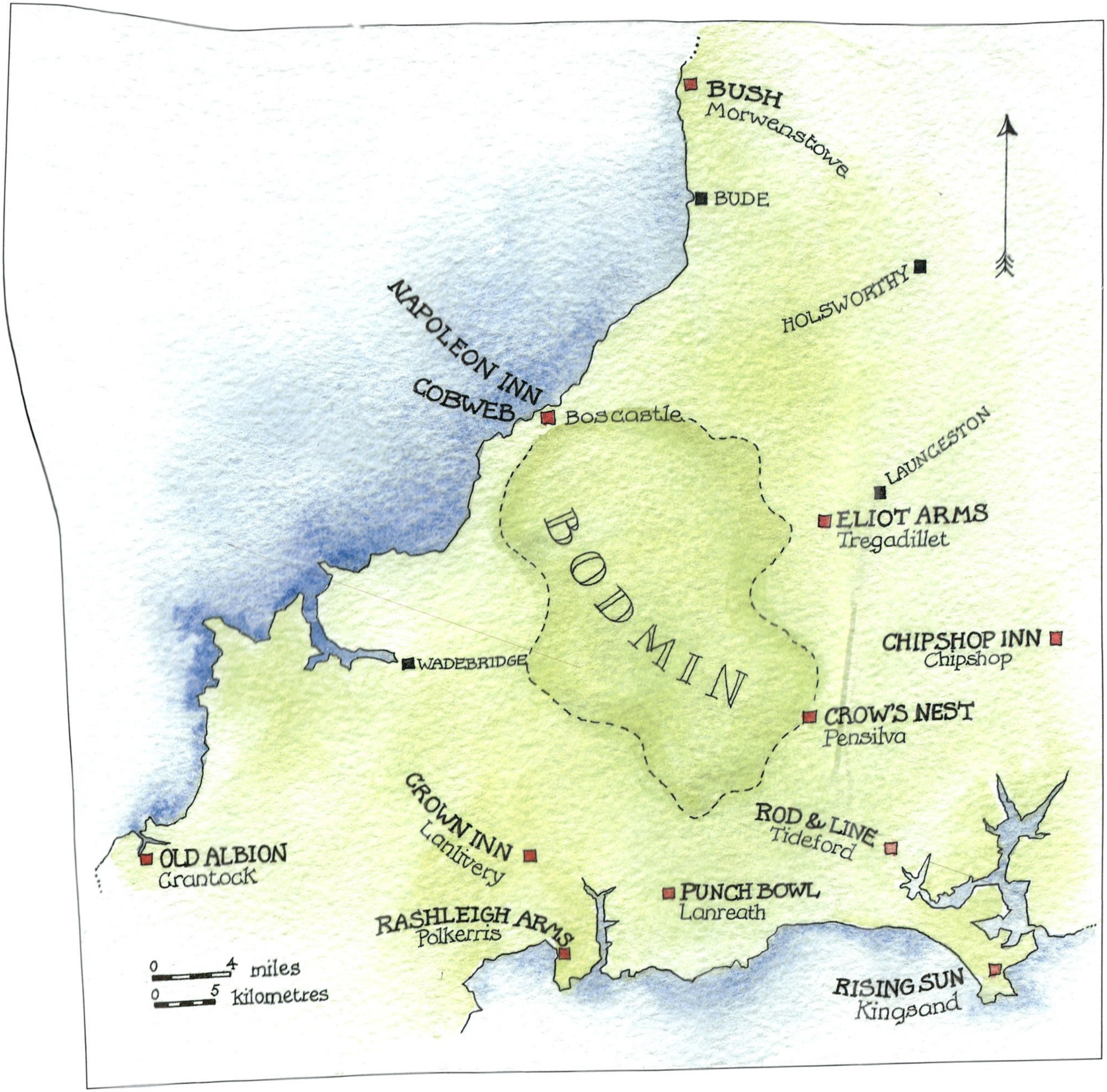
BUSH
Morwenstowe
BUDE
HOLSWORTHY
NAPOLEON INN
COBWEB
Boscastle
LAUNCESTON
ELIOT ARMS
Tregadillet
BODMIN
WADEBRIDGE
CHIPSHOP INN
Chipshop
CROW'S NEST
Pensilva
CROWN INN
Lanlivery
ROD & LINE
Tideford
OLD ALBION
Crantock
PUNCH BOWL
Lanreath
RASHLEIGH ARMS
Polkerris
RISING SUN
Kingsand
0 4 miles
0 5 kilometres

East Cornwall

BUSH INN

Morwenstowe

Signposted from A39, north of Bude.

Most visitors to Morwenstowe head for the church, once the domain of Cornwall's most famous and eccentric parson, the Rev Stephen Hawker, who was parson here for forty years during the last century. He built his grand vicarage using his own money and the chimneys were designed to replicate the towers of parish churches in which he had worked. One chimney represents his mother's tomb. It was a rather expensive folly which left him poor for the rest of his life, but never curbed his eccentric behaviour.

The coastline here has claimed many victims over the years, and in the churchyard is the figurehead of the sailing ship Caledonia on which all but one of the crew perished. The Rev Hawker located all the bodies and gave them a decent burial. Although he died a hundred years ago, some believe that Hawker still visits the Bush Inn, if only in spirit form. The old place is certainly renowned for a few ghostly visitors.

Many pubs lay claim to being the oldest in the land. The Bush has more reason than most. Parts of the building are said to date back a thousand years when it was used as a hermits' cell. Hermits, of course, had an obsession about isolating themselves from the rest of the world and, in those days, it would have been hard to pick a more remote location. It still feels remote, even with the main north coast trunk road running just a few miles away.

It would be easy to miss the pub on the way down to the church. Set behind a village green (actually

it's not a village green as there is no village to speak of, but it looks as if it ought to be) the pub appears as an ordinary complex of farm buildings with only a simple sign to mark its presence. The sign itself is an indication of the age of the pub as the name The Bush dates back to the time of the Romans. When they borrowed our country for a few centuries they brought with them their tavernas to keep their marauding troops happy. These forerunners of the modern roadside pub were marked by hanging a bush outside the front door.

In the 13th century the Bush was home to a group of Cistercian monks. In one wall of the main bar is the Piscina where the monks used to wash their chalices.

Up to about forty years ago this was a working farm as well as a pub. The top bar, The Shippen Bar, was where the cows were kept. Going back further, there was once a leper colony in Morwenstowe, and a narrow slit in the wall by the entrance is known as the lepers' squint as it was here that they apparently peeked through to see what the monks were up to inside.

There are those who believe that the Bush is the real Jamaica Inn immortalised by Daphne du Maurier. The writer used to live in nearby Kilkhampton and when searching for inspiration for a smugglers' pub it seems to make more sense that it would be set here, on the coast, rather than in the middle of Bodmin Moor.

Real Ales: St. Austell.

TALES FROM THE SNUG

Over the centuries drinkers have invented all manner of mixtures to spice up their beer. They include such delights as: Humpty Dumpty, a gypsy drink made from ale boiled with brandy; a Dog's Nose, made of warm porter, sugar, gin and nutmeg; Lamb's Wool, an old beverage consisting of apple juice boiled with ale, sugar and nutmeg; and Cup, a mixture of strong ale, sugar, spice and lemon served in a silver cup… "he was in his cups".

CHIPSHOP INN

Chipshop

In the middle of nowhere, off the A384, about 3 miles west of Tavistock.

Witty remarks about fish'n'chips are probably not appreciated here. They have heard them all before. This Chipshop has absolutely nothing to do with Harry Ramsden emporiums or the like.

The pub was once perfectly described as "An isolated building standing at a country crossroads on the road from nowhere to somewhere smaller… a curious place to find a successful drinking establishment." Curious indeed, but a couple of hundred years ago this place was at the centre of a busy mining area. Just up the road was the Devon Great Consules, said to be the biggest copper mine

in the world. The mine-workers were paid with tokens or chips which could then be exchanged for various goods throughout the local community. It was a clever business ploy by the mine owners, who also happened to own most of the local shops and ale-houses. Thus, with one hand they paid their men with chips, and with the other hand they grabbed them back through their shops. They couldn't lose. The place soon renamed itself after the chip system.

It's believed the pub dates back to the late 18th century when it was a farm, barn, brewery and local store. A one-bar pub, it has a good reputation for real ale. Landlord Tim Pattermore always has three or four ales on offer, and regularly introduces guest ales, so that in any one year a local drinker could work through sixty or seventy different beers. One good reason for moving to Chipshop.

If you turn up at the pub in a classic car you are assured of a particular welcome as Tim also happens to be a serious enthusiast, which makes him OK by me.

Real Ales: Bass, Emoor, guest ales.

TALES FROM THE SNUG

During the eighteenth and nineteenth centuries the nobility prided themselves on the amount they could drink, and there was a great deal of boasting about the number of bottles consumed at one sitting. Thus the expression 'drunk as a lord' came into being.

TALES FROM THE SNUG

There was a time, not so long ago, when every bar in the country had a big-busted barmaid pulling pints and listening to the customers' troubles. There are those who believe that the age of easy-to-pour keg beers, the Red Barrel Period, was responsible for the demise of these wonderful people. The New Statesman at the time summed it up with:

> *"Not turning taps but pulling pumps gave barmaids splendid busts and rumps."*

COBWEB

Boscastle

In the heart of the town opposite the main car park.

As any sailor probably knows, there are not many safe harbours on the North Cornwall and North Devon coast. Boscastle is one of the few, and, even then, only for those in the know. It is not the easiest port to enter or leave. However, a few hundred years ago the lovely little port of Boscastle would have been brim full of sailing vessels bringing cargoes from all round Britain and Europe. They would arrive with essential supplies for the surrounding communities, and leave with cargoes of slate, grain and china clay.

When the railways came in the late 19th century the ships gradually disappeared, and today it is only the occasional visiting yachtsmen who makes the tricky entrance to the harbour. In those days the port used to have something like eighteen pubs, (nowadays it's only three) but they weren't all pubs then, they were beer houses or kiddlywink taverns. (For an explanation Kiddleywinks, see the Lamorna Wink). It's one of those coastal towns which seems to have escaped the worst excesses of the tourist market, since most visitors tend to head on further west, to the brasher attractions of Tintagel with all its Arthurian souvenir and gift shops.

Gone are the days when pubs were places of sticky carpets smelling of stale beer and cigarette ash. Nowadays they tend to pong a bit of polish and air freshener and all those funny little pink things you put down the lavatory bowls. The Cobweb used to make a positive virtue of the fact that it hadn't seen a duster for years, and got its name from the fact that it was once covered in the things.

Until the middle of this century the place was a store house for wine and flour. It first got a licence back in 1790 in the days when ships arriving in Boscastle harbour brought with them cargoes of wine and spirits. No doubt not all of it was declared to the Customs men and the odd bit of smuggled grog got through. The place was more of a 'jug and bottle' than a pub. Customers would come with their own large pots and jars to buy wine and spirits for drinking at home. Dozens of these pots decorate the walls and beams of the Cobweb today.

The cobwebs in the pub were originally encouraged, as they were home to the spiders which fed on the vinegar flies which would otherwise turn the wine sour. When the place became a proper pub in 1947, the landlord saw no reason to get rid of the cobwebs. Visitors thought it was quaint, so much so that over the years they practically denuded the place as they kept pinching the cobwebs as souvenirs of their visit. What they did with them when they got home is anybody's guess. Peer closely into the dark corners and you can still find them, but it's not like it was in days past.

While part of the Cobweb has been transformed into a dining area, it still keeps a proper drinkers' bar, stone floor, large wooden settles, beer from the barrel and, of course, cobwebs.

Real Ales: St Austell, Bass, Abbots.

TALES FROM THE SNUG

By the late 16th century there was approximately one ale house for every 142 inhabitants. Today the figure is about one pub for 6,000 inhabitants.

Hostel and workshop for disabled
Disabled people
The Crown
FREE HOUSE
GOOD FOOD

CROWN INN

Lanlivery

A couple of miles west of Lostwithiel - look for the sign off the A390.

The peaceful village of Lanlivery lies on the old Saints Way, the path which runs from Padstow in the north to Fowey in the south. In Medieaval times the path was used by drovers, seamen and Christian missionaries on their way to spread the Word in France. In those days it was considered safer to walk across the peninsula than to risk the stormy seas surrounding Lands End.

The path was at its busiest between the 6th and 10th centuries, which pre-dates the Crown, but, no doubt even then, the walkers stopped off in Lanlivery for some kind of refreshment. Nevertheless, The Crown remains one of the oldest pubs in Cornwall, believed to date back to the 12th century.

The main bar through the entrance is stone floored with interesting cubby holes and alcoves for the more private conversation. There is a small back bar much favoured by the locals, and a dining area. The pub also has a very pleasant garden for those who prefer to imbibe outdoors.

One of The Crown's more notorious customers was Jan Tregeagle, the steward of Lanhydrock who, by all accounts, was not a very nice chap at all. He murdered his wife and children and went on to marry - and murder - a number of rich ladies of Cornwall. The story goes that after a night's drinking with the Devil, who just happened to have popped into the Crown for a snifter, Tregeagle sold his soul to old Lucifer for yet more cash.

A ballad of 1807 recalls the night:

"A bargaine, A bargaine", said he aloude,
"At my lot I will never repyne;
I swear to observe it, I sweare by the roode,
And am readye to seale and to synge with my bloode,
Bothe my soule and my bodye are thyne!"

Perhaps it is to keep the Devil away that the church next to the pub has one of the few eight bell set-ups in the county. The bell-ringers are regulars at The Crown on practice night.

By the 1920s Lanlivery was a stronghold of Methodism, and the villagers even went to the trouble of buying the pub in order to close it down. It remained a private house until the seventies when, to the relief of many, it was re-opened as a pub.

Real Ales: Bass, Sharp's.

CROW'S NEST

Pensilva

Off the B3254 between Pensilva and St Cleer.

This part of east Cornwall has been attracting settlers since the Stone Age, but the highspot of its long history came when rich desposits of copper, tin and arsenic were discovered in the surrounding hills. In the 17th century the miners moved in, and up until the early 20th century, the area enjoyed wealth far beyond that which agriculture had provided.

The pub in Crow's Nest was the old Mine Captain's pay house. The mine owners controlled almost all aspects of life in the village, with the miners being paid in Crows Nest Tokens. These could be exchanged in the village for all goods and services which, in turn, were also owned by the mine. It may sound very feudal but the system - similar to the one which operated in Chipshop - worked well, and everyone was well looked after.

The villagers of today are proud of their mining history, and the pub arranges regular talks on the subject. There is an old bell outside the pub with which the Mine Captain used to summon the men to collect their pay. It's a safe bet that some of their tokens found their way back across the counter in exchange for beer.

The low ceiling of the pub is festooned not, as you might expect, with miners' lamps and industrial bits and pieces, but by all things horsey. It is an amazing collection of snaffles, bridles and other contraptions which go in horses' mouths. Customers have brought them in over the years and the collection continues to grow.

The Crow's Nest has its residents from the spirit world, including one ghost who manifests himself by a dreadful smell, apparently something akin to decomposing flesh. He is believed to have been some unfortunate chap who got himself buried in the priest hole, a tunnel which leads from the pub to the chapel. Another of the pub's ghosts is a young girl in a bridal gown. It is said that she was trying on the gown in what was then the landlord's sitting room, when news came through that her fiance had been drowned in a mining accident.

This all sounds very sad and sombre, but I have always found the pub to have an atmosphere which is quite the opposite.

Real Ales: St Austell.

TALES FROM THE SNUG

"As much of the history of England has been brought about in public-houses as in the House of Commons."
(Sir William Harcourt) 1872

ELIOT ARMS

Tregadillet

3 miles west of Launceston, signposted off the A30.

Not so long ago the attractive, ivy-clad Eliot Arms was in an enviable position for a pub, on the edge of the busy main road into Cornwall, ideally placed to attract the thirsty traveller, but then they built a by-pass. All very convenient for the motorist in a hurry but not too good for business.

Today the village of Tregadillet is a quiet place and the Eliot Arms has had to work hard to attract trade. Landlord John Cooke has done it by turning the pub into a kind of Old Curiosity Shop. The place is stuffed full of antiques, and it is these as much as the good food and beer which make the place well worth a detour off the by-pass.

The Eliot Arms is also called the Square and Compass and known to the locals as just 'The Compass'. John is keen to keep alive the tradition of the pub having two names. The Eliot bit is from the name of a Liskeard landowner, and the Square & Compass derives from its Masonic connections. After the Napoleonic Wars, some French prisoners of war worked on the fields around Tregadillet while others were busy building their own prison on the middle of Dartmoor. Even as prisoners they retained their Freemasonry dealings. The pub was used for Lodge meetings.

The place is crammed full of curios. Even the dining tables and chairs make up an assortment of well used and loved furniture, rather than being of the usual bland brewery design.

Time at the Eliot Arms can be called from any one of ninety or so clocks which adorn the place, but, for the sake of residents, the chime has been removed from most of them. Old prints, books, china, cigarette cards - it's a collector's paradise.

There are, of course, also horse brasses which date back to the age of coaching inns. The coaches have long since disappeared, but owners of country pubs persist in the belief that they can't be real country pubs without at least a string or two of the things hanging from the walls. I am sure there must be a factory in the Far East churning out brasses in the sure knowledge that they will never go anywhere near a horse, but will end up on a pub wall. The Eliot has a thousand horse brasses, and a very patient cleaning lady who polishes them all regularly.

Snuff taking was once common, but now all that remains of the habit are the boxes, and the Eliot Arms has four hundred of them.

I am sure if some brewery accountant looked closely at the Eliot Arms he would pretty quickly realise that by getting rid of some of the antiques there would be room for a lot more customers, but brewery accountants tend not to understand the finer points of pub culture!

Real Ales: St Austell, and Dartmoor Best.

TALES FROM THE SNUG

The popular pub game of cribbage was invented by a seventeenth century poet called Sir John Suckling. Having invented it, he turned it to his advantage by playing with marked cards and making a fortune which would be worth £4 million today.

NAPOLEON INN

Boscastle

At the top end of the town.

The good people of Boscastle have been drinking in this pub for around 450 years, although when it was first licensed back in1543 it was known, for some reason, as The Shilling. Back then beer was of very unpredictable nature and the beer to be found in Cornwall had a particularly bad reputation. Round about this time the writer Andrew Boorde quoted a rhyme on Cornish ale:

"Ich am a Cornish man, ale I can brew
It will make one to cackle, also to spew,
It is thick and smokey and also it is thin.
It is like wash as pigs had wrestled therein."

Things are better now (though I must confess I am not a great fan of one or two of the commonest beers to be found in the county).

It wasn't until about 200 years ago that the pub really started getting busy. That was the time when Napoleon was giving us all sorts of trouble on the Continent and we were rapidly running short of soldiers and sailors, so this pub became one of the many recruiting centres set up around the country.

I don't imagine they were exactly queuing up in the streets to volunteer for this, so the British Army came up with this great scheme, whereby from about 1800 all British soldiers and NCOs were offered a penny a day in lieu of their beer allowance. It became known as beer money, an expression which has stayed with us. Not much of an incentive to volunteer and go off to almost certain death.

Death, destruction, ancient walls steeped in history, it came as no surprise to hear that the pub had a ghost or three, according to landlord Richard Claridge. One of them stands and looks through the serving hatch in the side bar. He has long flowing hair, big cuffs on his sleeves, and he just hovers there, keeping an eye on things in the next bar.

The back bar of The Nap is regularly taken over by some very talented musicians who drop in for impromptu jam sessions.

Going back a few years, customers would regularly take home a bottle or two of beer. There was a threepenny deposit on the bottle, but the landlord made the mistake of storing the empties at the back of the pub. Locals who were short of drinking money would simply sneak round to collect an armful of bottles, pop into the bar, collect the deposit money, and drink free for the evening. That doesn't happen any more.

Real Ales: St. Austell ales.

TALES FROM THE SNUG

Britain's brewers produce around thirteen million gallons of beer per year, but that still only puts us in second place in terms of European beer production. German brewers produce nearly twice as much. In third place are the Spanish, who produce a mere five and a half million gallons a year. (Brewers and Licensed Retailers Association, 1999)

TALES FROM THE SNUG

Before the days of refrigeration, the brewing industry went very quiet during the summer months when warm weather made the fermentation and conditioning of beer a difficult operation. Ale was still produced, but the quality left much to be desired. Drinkers looked forward to September which is traditionally the start of the new brewing season, and many breweries still celebrate the month with the production of special September Ales.

OLD ALBION

Crantock

Signposted off the A3075, a couple of miles west of Newquay.

Legend has it that back in the mists of time there was a large community not far from present day Crantock, in a village called Langurroc. It was home to a collegiate foundation and no less than seven churches, but this didn't stop the locals falling into bad habits and all manner of evil activities. As a punishment for their sins, one day there came a mighty sandstorm and the whole village simply disappeared beneath the sands. Nobody seems too sure exactly where to find the remains of Langurroc, which is remarkable for such a big place, but it makes a good story.

Crantock itself is named after one St Carantocus, an Irish man who built a church here. Nowadays the village tends to be overshadowed by its brash neighbour Newquay, but half a millenium ago it was the other way round. Crantock was a busy port and Newquay was a mere hamlet known as Towan Blistra.

The Old Albion dates back almost to this time of great prosperity, and gets its name from a famous ship of the day. Needless to say it was the headquarters of the local smuggling fraternity who made use of a tunnel now hidden beneath the carpet by the fireplace. It's thought the tunnel runs under the village to connect with The Ship Inn.

There is a saying about Cornish miners which suggests that there is no hole in the ground anywhere in the world without a Cornishman being down it. It does seem, if all the stories are to true, that Cornish smugglers could not get the mining bug out of their bones and spent a great deal of their time digging tunnels in and out of their local pubs.

Real Ales: Skinner's, Courage Best, guest ales.

TALES FROM THE SNUG

During the Middle Ages there was a fashion for sharing drinking vessels marked with wooden pegs set at intervals down the length of the tankard. The tankard would be passed around the table and each drinker would quaff down the ale as far as the next peg, thus ensuring that everyone got a fair share. With individual drinking vessels, if the landlord felt the drinker had had enough, he would start rationing his ale by "taking him down a peg".

PUNCH BOWL

Lanreath

Signposted off the B3359, north of Polperro.

The Punch Bowl is probably Cornwall's largest coaching inn to survive from the days when horsepower meant just that. Once upon a time it also served as the village court house, with accused and accuser having their own rooms (now separate bars) at the front while the judge held court at the back. The courtroom has been converted into a smart dining room.

This is a pub with more than its fair share of legends and stories, some of which may even be true.

One of the most intriguing concerns an old rector of the church who was married to a younger woman. He made the mistake of taking on a young curate and, inevitably, the wife decided that the newcomer was rather more attractive than her husband. The affair developed until one day the old rector was found dead under mysterious circumstances. At the same moment a black cockerel appeared in the village and began terrorising the locals who believed that the Devil had turned the old man into the bird.

Things reached a height when the villagers ganged together and chased the cockerel through the streets. In panic the bird flew through the kitchen window of the Punch Bowl and hid in an oven next to the fire. A big mistake, that. The terrified kitchen maid slammed the door of the oven shut and it has never been opened from that day to this.
One or two locals believe that the cockerel still haunts the pub and frightens the life out of visitors by tapping them on the shoulder. Of course, the whole story could be proved one way or the other if somebody were to take a peek into the oven to see if any chicken bones remain, but nobody dares.

On a less evil note, the parish saint, St Marnarch, is said to have stayed at the Punch Bowl and blessed the pub's well which, thereafter, had miraculous properties, but they can't have been too special as, during one refurbishment, the well was covered up and now languishes beneath the floor of the ladies' loo.

Charles II also stayed here (if all the claims are true, then Charles spent nearly all his reign riding from pub to pub throughout the country, leaving very little time to do any governing). He apparently left the Punch Bowl in a hurry by jumping out of his window straight into the saddle of his horse and galloping off across the hills.

Another distinguished guest at the inn was the artist Augustus John who did at least leave behind some proof of his visit. He designed the elaborate pub sign which hangs above the entrance.

Real Ales: Bass, Sharp's Doom Bar, Sharp's Own.

TALES FROM THE SNUG

By 1700 all ale was made with hops. There was a growing preference for very strong beers highly malted and stored for up to five years. Many beers were flavoured with herbs, spices and other less appetising ingredients. One popular drink in the early 18th century was Cock Ale, a particular favourite of whores and rogues, prepared by steeping raisins, dates nutmegs and a newly killed cock in a cask of beer.

RASHLEIGH INN
Rashleigh Inn

RASHLEIGH ARMS

Polkerris

Signposted off the A3082, between Fowey and St Blazey.

I have been to lots of so-called 'waterfront pubs' only to be let down on discovering that between the pub and the water is a busy road, a railway line or some other distraction, but when the Rashleigh Arms says 'waterfront', it really means it. It is as close to the sea as it is possible to be... indeed, with a high tide and a strong wind, it can find itself right in the stuff.

Polkerris is a small hamlet overlooking St Austell Bay, and a hundred years ago this was a busy little fishing port earning a good living from the pilchard shoals which obligingly turned up regularly every year. The fishermen quenched their thirsts in a pub called the General Elliot which was right next to the coastguard station.

A great storm washed away the General Elliot, and the drinkers eventually converted the coastguard station into a pub which was named after the Rashleigh family. They were owners of much of the land around Polkerris including Menabilly, the mansion made famous as 'Manderley' by Daphne du Maurier in her novel "Rebecca". The novelist lived for a time in Kilmarth, another mansion overlooking Polkerris.

Where once around two hundred people in Polkerris earned a living from fishing, today the main source of income is tourism. At the height of the season this is a very popular spot, and at its centre is the Rashleigh Arms. A lesser pub might capitalise unashamedly on the tourist trade, but the Rashleigh still manages to feel like a proper 'local' serving proper beer. It also has an excellent reputation for its food, with a separate dining area so that consumers of solids do not interfere with those sticking to a liquid diet.

Another major point in the pub's favour is the upright piano. Not too long ago, most pubs had a piano in the corner, and there was always someone prepared to hammer out a few tunes for a good old fashioned sing-song. What the pianist lacked in musical ability was usually more than compensated for by enthusiasm. Gradually the pianos were replaced with juke boxes and muzak machines, so that now they are rarer than hairs on an egg. Mercifully, a few pubs still realise their value, and the piano at the Rashleigh gets used regularly.

Real Ales: Bass, Tanglefoot, Otter, St Austell.

RISING SUN

Kingsand

The best way to arrive here is to take the Cremyll Ferry from Plymouth and stroll through the gardens of Mount Edgcumbe. The pub is the first one you come to in Kingsand.

They call this the 'forgotten corner of Cornwall' because it is a long way from the usual tourist route west and, consequently, it takes a bit of effort to get there. Happily, this has meant that, to a large extent, the village remains refreshingly unspoilt.

Standing watch over the south western entrance to Plymouth Sound, the villagers of Kingsand and neighbouring Cawsand have traditionally earned their living from the sea. This is where fishermen would subsidise their earnings by piloting ships into Plymouth, and of course with a bit of smuggling on the side. They lived cheek by jowl with customs and revenue men who did their best to curb the more illegal activities.

The Rising Sun dates back to the mid-eighteenth century, when it is thought that it was used as a Customs House. A century later, the customs men moved out, and the fishermen moved in, when the building was changed into a pub. It hasn't looked back since.

Fishing in those days had its seasons. There was a time for pilchards, a time for herring, shellfish and so on. There were also the hard times when catches were poor. For those occasions, a 'stocker pot' was kept behind the bar at the Rising Sun. Every time a fisherman was paid for his catch, the money was shared out between the crew, with a share for the boat, and an additional share for the stocker pot. When money was short, they could still get a drink at the pub by dipping into the pot.

Despite the reference to 'the forgotten corner…', this part of Cornwall hasn't been totally ignored by tourists, and there are now a large number of holiday cottages in the village which means that winters can be very quiet. However, the Rising Sun is a friendly little pub, well supported by the locals. And even in the depths of winter there are hardy walkers around who will find a welcoming log fire and a good pint.

Real Ales: Bass, Courage Best, and a guest ale.

ROD AND LINE

Tideford

(See below for directions).

The busy A38 through Cornwall is not the most attractive road in the country. It's one of those functional thoroughfares with little in the way of picturesque villages or stunning countryside to distract the driver. Consequently, everyone uses it as nothing more than a means of getting to their destination as soon as possible, with no hesitation or deviation. If they did but know it, just a short way off the main road there are some very worthwhile watering holes to be discovered.

Tideford, meaning no disrespect, is the sort of village which at first glance has little to encourage the traveller to stop, but less than a hundred yards from where the traffic rushes by is a simple pub with a great local atmosphere, the Rod and Line. Hereinafter the pub should, perhaps, be called the Rod and Ine, since the 'L' on the pub's sign had mysteriously disappeared when we went to take the photograph!

There always seems to be a good crowd of locals and a lot of laughs to be had, which proves once again that a pub is as good as the landlord behind the bar. Mike Jones is a landlord who obviously enjoys the job, a quality that's disappointingly rare.

There are often things going on at the Rod and Line, with celebrations at the slightest excuse. St. Perran's Night is one of the traditional parties (well, 'traditional' in so much as it was started in 1998 and was so successful that it looks like becoming an annual occasion!)

St. Perran would greatly approve of the event as, according to the stories, he was not averse to downing the odd glass of happy juice. He was thrown out of Ireland, literally. A millstone was tied around his neck and he was chucked off a cliff, but the millstone miraculously turned into a boat, and he floated across the water to wash up on the shores of Cornwall. There, he lit a fire, and upon that fire he placed a black rock, no doubt mistaking it for a lump of coal in his befuddlement. From this coal there began to issue a stream of white molten metal. Lo and behold, St Perran had discovered tin. The Cornish flag, a white cross on a black background, is supposed to commemorate the occasion. Pretty soon there was a thriving tin industry and the miners elected Perran to be their patron saint. He died, the legend says, while enjoying a bit of drunken revelry at the age of 206 years.

Well, I believe it.

The good Saint P. would like the Rod and Line. The highspot of the celebrations is the pasty competition in which the locals bring in their creations to be judged by a panel of experts which includes the local butcher (now retired, but whose reputation for excellent meat made the butcher's shop in Tideford another good reason to stop off there). The subject of what makes a good pasty is one which constantly comes up in conversation in Cornish pubs. Older Cornish folk have pretty fixed and positive views about the real traditional pasty, but on St Perran's night it has to be said that the first and fourth prizes went to complete novices who had never made one in their lives before.

While on the subject of meat, there is another good reason to drop in at the Rod and Line. Mike, the landlord, is an enthusiastic (if not always successful) member of a local shooting syndicate, and the Game Pie he produces for the pub is worth travelling for.

Real Ales: Ushers Best, Founders.

TALES FROM THE SNUG

Local magistrates controlled prices through the ale-tasters. In 1574 Robert Laneham described the typical ale-taster as one who as ' ever acquitted himself with such estimation… his judgement will be taken above the best in the parish, be his nose never so red.'

ISLES OF SCILLY
St. Agnes
St. Mary's
ATLANTIC
BISHOP & WOLF
MERMAID
TURKS HEAD
NEWQUAY
TINNERS ARMS
Zennor
SLOOP INN
St. Ives
CAMBORNE
REDRUTH
TRURO
ROSELAND INN
Philleigh
PANDORA INN
Restronguet Creek
WHITE HART
Ludgvan
STAR INN
St. Just
PENZANCE
BLUE ANCHOR
Helston
TRELOWARREN ARMS
Budock Water
SEVEN STARS
Falmouth
FIVE PILCHARDS
Porthallow
LAMORNA WINK
Lamorna
LOGAN ROCK
Treen
HALZEPHRON
Gunwalloe
CADGWITH COVE INN
Cadgwith
0 4 miles
0 5 kilometres

West Cornwall & The Isles of Scilly

BLUE ANCHOR

Helston, Cornwall

Coinagehall Street.

Helston originally developed around the tin industry, being one of the five medieval Stannary towns in Cornwall. It's hard to believe now, but seven hundred years ago this was quite a busy port for the export of tin, but then the River Cober became partially blocked by a shingle bank, and Helston took on a new life as a market town. In more recent times it has become host to countless servicemen based at nearby R.N.A.S. Culdrose, who ensure that the town's attractions are never short of customers.

The Blue Anchor at the bottom end of the main street is a 'must' for any dedicated pub hunter and beer lover. Such pubs were once commonplace but now are sadly few and far between.

In the fifteenth century this was a monks' rest-house. They would probably have brewed beer for their own benefit and for the occasional passing pilgrim. When Henry VIII wreaked his havoc in the monasteries, the monks were forced to turn brewing into a full time business, and beer has been brewed commercially here ever since. The Blue Anchor is one of only four brew-pubs in the country dating back so far. The brewery itself is at the back of the pub and now, as then, all ingredients have to be carried along the flag-stoned corridor that runs through the building. Just off this corridor are the two dark, low-ceilinged bars, constantly filled with locals who all know a good beer when they taste one.

All the beer brewed at the Blue Anchor comes under the title Spingo (a derivation of Stingo) and comes in three strengths. The weakest, confusingly called "Middle" is around 5% ABV, so this is not a beer for boys. It doesn't taste particularly strong so beware, it has a habit of creeping up and hitting you on the back of the neck and has been the downfall of many a poor drinker who has underestimated its power. For special occasions a stronger brew is produced…

around 7.6% ABV! There is a story that an American tourist managed to talk his way out of a drink/drive offence by pleading ignorance as to the strength of beer he had been drinking at the Blue Anchor. Don't risk it. Take it from me, it's strong.

The big day in Helston is "Furry Fair", a celebration of the time when the Devil once tried to take over the town but was defeated by St Michael. The original party got its name from 'fer', the old Cornish word for 'feast day' but now it is better known as Floral Day when the town echoes to the sound of the well-known Floral Dance. It takes place every year in early May and the celebrations begin early in the Blue Anchor. By tradition, the band which accompanies the all-day dancing pops into the pub for a heart-starter pint for breakfast, the first of many such pints downed throughout the proceedings. It is not the best day to appreciate the pub in all its ancient glory. You will be lucky to get near the bar, for a start.

Real Ale: Spingo!

TALES FROM THE SNUG

Brewing ale in the early days was a hazardous occupation. The process involved boiling water which meant open fires and, at a time when most houses were constructed of wood, there were incidents of ale-houses burning to the ground. The situation was so bad in London that in the 12th century it was decreed that all ale-houses in the City should be constructed of stone. As a result, ale was in short supply for many years.

TALES FROM THE SNUG

While Britain lies second in the European league of beer producers, we are back in fifth position when it comes to drinking it. We spend more than £15 billion a year on beer, but our total consumption amounts to an average of less than half a pint a day per head. We are currently being beaten in the league table by Germany, Ireland, Denmark and Austria, in that order. (Brewers and Licensed Retailers Association, 1999)

CADGWITH COVE INN

Cadgwith

In Helston take the A3083 road to the Lizard. Cadgwith is signposted to the left shortly before you drop off the end of England.

If the film producers of Hollywood ever want to design what they think of as a typical Cornish fishing village, they do it along the lines of Cadgwith. A narrow road winds its way down the hill into the village through whitewashed thatched and slate-roofed cottages. Fishing boats lie waiting on the beach for the next tide and, of course, there is a fine old Cornish pub waiting to welcome the thirsty traveller.

Cadgwith is still very much a working village, as testified by the fishing boats which may be fewer in number nowadays, but are still earning a living from the sea. The boats provide the pub with a ready supply of wonderfully fresh crab, lobster and mackerel. A hundred years ago it would have been pilchards, pilchards and more pilchards, but these fish have found some other waters in which to spend their holidays, and there are now only a few old cellars and store-rooms in the village as a reminder of this most lucrative part of the local fishing industry.

Many Cornish coastal villages have surrendered to the invasion of tourism, with the result that old cottages have been turned into desirable holiday homes, souvenir shops and Cream Tea Rooms. In Cadgwith, while there is a growing number of holiday homes, the place remains quintessentially Cornish and is all the better for it. I am sure that one reason for this is the fact that visitors have to park their cars at the top of the village and walk down to the Cove, which tends to puts off the less energetic.

Even so, in the summer season Cadgwith is extremely popular, and the pub does a roaring trade with standing room only in the small bar and on the terrace. To add to the attraction of the place there is live music on some evenings, and a regular Friday night session where the locals get together as a choir. It is not a formally organised choir and tends to vary in size according to who turns up for a drink, but very good they are!

While other parts of England had 'spit and sawdust' pubs, the Cadgwith Cove Inn, like many Cornish boozers, was a 'spit and sand', the sand being more readily available, and cheaper, whilst serving exactly the same purpose. The sand has long since been swept away and the spittoons removed, but little else has changed here and it is well worth the walk from the car park.

REAL ALES: Bass, Sharp's and guest ales.

FIVE PILCHARDS

Porthallow

Lies on the eastern shore of the Lizard Peninsula, a couple of miles north of St. Keverne.

Porthallow, or Pralla as the locals call it, was once the home of a thriving pilchard fishing industry. When the fish were plentiful, the boats landed their catch on the beach and they were salted and prepared in the building next to the pub. An annual Pilchard Supper used to be held in the room above the pub and was no doubt one of the main social events of the year in Porthallow.

The pilchards have long since disappeared, but their memory lives on in the pub, the Five Pilchards. No-one is quite sure of the significance of the 'five'.

There is a story that it was once called Three Pilchards, but everyone got confused with another local pub called the Three Tuns, so the landlord added a couple more.

Today's landlord, Brandon Flyn, knows exactly what Cornish drinkers want in a pub, having previously run the Shipwrights in Helford and the Mermaid on St Mary's. The result is that the Five Pilchards remains pleasantly basic, a proper pub. Proof of that is its popularity with the locals, some of whom were born and bred in the village. Lily is one such local and, aged 75 when I met her, she still works regularly in the pub. There must be something in the beer in Porthallow, as there are several septuagenarians and octogenarians who use the pub and they all appear far younger than their actual years.

The Five Pilchards has a thriving group of euchre players. It's an old pub card game which I have never been able to understand despite numerous attempts to explain the rules to me.

There's live music on occasions, all very impromptu and all the better for it.

Real Ales: London Pride, Abbot Ale, Sharp's.

TALES FROM THE SNUG

Monks, particularly those in the West Country, were enthusiastic cider makers and believed the apple tree to have religious significance. During the Middle Ages they even used cider to baptise babies.

HALZEPHRON

Gunwalloe

Take the A3083 south of Helston and dive off west to explore the shore of the Lizard Peninsula.

The wild coastline and cliffs of the Lizard Peninsula have long been a source of stories of storms and shipwrecks and smugglers. They called them "the cliffs of hell" which in the old Cornish language was Als Yfferin. Try saying that after a glass or two of the oh-be-joyful. Halzephron rolls off the tongue a bit more easily, and it accounts for the strangely named pub to be found above those cliffs at Gunwalloe.

The Halzephron was built around five hundred years ago. Once a simple roadside inn, the pub has had a chequered history, going through a variety of good and not so good owners. The previous owners only opened the pub on two nights a week, but in 1993 it was reopened, refurbished and refreshed. It's now gained a fine reputation for the standard of its food and ales, and the pub walls are covered with prestigious awards.

The Halzephron used to be known as The Ship and it was no doubt the centre of a thriving smuggling and wrecking business in the area. A tunnel leads from the shore below to a secret shaft, which emerges in the attic of the pub. Illicit booze used to be brought in by the barrel load, and the revenue men never knew a single thing about it. The shaft is now hidden behind a wall in the bar.

For many years this century the Halzephron reverted to being just a farmhouse. Then in 1958 a well known local character, John Mills, got together with a few farmers and persuaded the Kerrier Brewster Sessions that it was vitally important there should be a pub again in the area. This wasn't for the benefit of the local drinkers, but in case there should be a sick sheep requiring a drop of brandy. There can't be many licences in Britain granted for the benefit of sheep.

Landlady Angela Thomas, as well as being a first class cook, is also a leading figure in operatic circles, and she bursts into song at the drop of a chef's hat. The sound of "The Floral Dance" can often be heard from the kitchen!

Out front the serious business of beer goes on. Local ales like Sharpe's Traditional, Doom Bar and Dartmoor Best.

TALES FROM THE SNUG

It was apparently a shipwreck that led to our liking for I.P.A., or India Pale Ale. The stuff used to be brewed purely for export to the British forces serving in India. One ship carrying the brew sank and crates of ale were washed ashore. We liked it so much that we demanded it be sold in this country as well.

LAMORNA WINK

Lamorna

Signposted off B3315 about 3 miles south west of Newlyn.

This was one of many Kiddley Wink drinking houses in Cornwall when smuggling was a way of life.

Some houses were licensed to sell beer and beer alone, but customers often desired something a little stronger. There was no shortage of smuggled brandy in the county, and the dodgy landlords of beer houses would hide the illicit spirit in the kitchen kettle. This was apparently enough to fool the Customs men but, of course, the locals knew all about it. They would come into the ale-house, wink in the general direction of the kettle, and be poured their slug of illegal booze. Hence, kettle and wink, which became kiddley wink. At least, that's the story! I can't help thinking that tiddley wink must also, in some way, be connected to the yarn.

Just getting to this pub is a delight, lying as it does in a beautiful wooded valley running down to the famous Lamorna Cove. The countryside here has always been an inspiration for writers and artists, many of whom set up studios in the area, and were regulars at the pub. Today many of the cottages are holiday homes which, in a way, reverts back to the time when the village was called Nantewas, meaning "the summering place".

At one end of the valley is a circle of stones known as the Merry Maidens. These, according to the story, were a group of excited girls who made the mistake of having a bit of a party on the Sabbath. As they danced there was a flash of lightning and they were all turned to stone. A bit steep really considering their 'crime'.

At the other end, in Lamorna Cove, is a rock where a mermaid is said to sit and sing alluringly. She is supposed to be responsible for the disappearance of several young men, not to mention the odd shipwreck.

The Lamorna Wink is an unpretentious pub, happily free of any false prettification. The bar is a bit like a museum of nautical memorabilia, with the walls and ceilings covered by a collection of intriguing bits and pieces ranging from ships crests to old diving helmets. The collection was started by the landlord's father around sixty years ago, and it is constantly receiving additions from interested customers.

Some regulars at the pub are of the four-legged furry variety! The landlord has for many years fed the wild foxes and badgers from the surrounding woodland, and the wily creatures know now that there is always a free supper if they turn up at the pub around closing time. Some are bold enough to wander into the bar, and many a customer has sworn to give up drink when realising he is sharing a table with a badger.

Real Ales: Flowers Best, Castle Eden.

TALES FROM THE SNUG

Up until the time of Henry VIII brewing and inn-keeping was very much under the control of the church, with monks providing bed, board and beer for travellers. After the dissolution of the monasteries the job was gradually taken over by the local squires and land-owning gentry. These were the first landlords. A new word had arrived in the drinkers' vocabulary.

LOGAN ROCK

Treen

Signposted off the B3315, about 6 miles before you drop off the end of England.

There are hundreds of Red Lions, Royal Oaks, New Inns and so on but there's only one Logan Rock. It's a friendly and unpretentious little pub on the South Cornish coast, just a few miles back from Lands End. Landlord Peter George is a well known local sportsman, so there's a lot of cricket talk in the bar. It's amazing how after just a few pints we tend to forget our beer bellies and general lack of fitness and become instant experts on the game, quietly hoping that no one asks us actually to play it.

The main attraction of the pub lies a pleasant walk away on the spectacular coast overlooking Porthcurno. In spring the cliffs are covered with wild flowers, the names of which escape me, but there are blue ones and yellow ones and pink ones and white ones. I did say that it was a pleasant stroll, but the last bit is harder going and eventually there it is, the Logan Rock itself.

This is one of the many Cornish logging stones which, through a freak of erosion over the centuries, ended up balancing precariously on a little pinnacle. Long before the days of theme parks, amusement arcades and entertainment complexes, these logging stones became big tourist attractions. In an age of simple pleasures it didn't seem to take much to amuse the visitors, and the locals made a penny or two by guiding them out to the rock and, no doubt, back to the pub for refreshment.

Then, in 1824, something happened which threatened to destroy their livelihood.
Until that time, the local story was that you could shift the rock just slightly with a fingertip, but no man could ever move it from its position. That is the kind of challenge which after a few pints some people find irresistible. So it was that one young Lieutenant Goldsmith and twelve of his cronies marched to the rock and somehow managed to dislodge it, sending it crashing into the crevice below. There was hell to pay from angry locals who insisted that it be replaced.

After much fuss Lieutenant Goldsmith was made, at his own expense, to come back and put the rock back exactly where he found it. It was a massive operation involving a large workforce and ingenious use of logs, ropes and pulleys, and it cost Lieutenant Goldsmith, nephew of the writer Oliver Goldsmith, a total of a hundred and thirty pounds, eight shillings and six pence, which was a lot of money back at the start of the nineteenth century. The people of Treen have dined out on the story ever since, and souvenirs of the occasion adorn the walls of the pub.

The granite boulders on the coast here hide a darker story too. The coast is said to have been the haunt of the St Levan Witches, a nice bunch of girls who gathered on the cliffs and cast spells to bring strong winds and a crop of ship wrecks to the rocks below. They do say even now that any woman coming down here at midnight and touching that Logan Rock nine times will turn immediately into a witch. Sounds like a huge effort to me and a similar effect can be achieved on a woman just by staggering home in an extra jolly mood two hours after closing time!

Real Ale: St. Austell.

MERMAID INN

St Mary's, Isles of Scilly

At the end of the quay, Hugh Town.

It is hard to mention one pub in St Marys without mentioning the others. There are three pubs, all within a few hundred yards of each other in the main street of Hugh Town, and drinkers tend to drift between them all. Half a century ago there were thirty pubs on St Mary's, but they were little more than small bars and drinking dens in the back of shops and farms. Things are more formalised nowadays.

The Mermaid is the first pub that visitors come across after stepping off the Scillonian ferry. It's a lovely trip, but it can be a bit wobbly on the legs, so many passengers feel the need for a quick reviver. Originallly this fine old solid stone building was a fishermen's store and warehouse. It was turned into a pub in the mid-fifties, and it's well used by the few fishermen still operating in the Scillies.

There was a time in the not so distant past when a brewery tried to make serious changes to the Mermaid, but the power of the locals is strong, and many of them boycotted the place until things were returned to normal. It is now back on form with the big main bar being a focal point for locals and visitors alike. The high ceilings and wooden walls are decorated with all manner of things to do with the sea, along with photographs of some of the local characters who have been known to sup the occasional ale here.

The Scillonians are a most hospitable bunch and they know how to enjoy themselves, particularly on gig-racing nights. There is always a lively atmosphere in the Mermaid and there is usuallly

someone prepared to burst into a song after a pint or two. The pub has a separate dining room which probably has the better views, but misses out on the fun.

Real Ales: Bass, Flowers.

Further along the street are two St Austell pubs, the oldest of which is **The Atlantic.** This began life as a row of cottages knocked into one, with a bar on the slipway. It was here that a local character apeared one day after an abortive shooting expedition. He was not too happy with his lack of success so he dropped a handful of live cartridges into the stove in the middle of the floor. The resulting series of explosions cleared the bar faster than any call of last orders!

Over the years the bar has moved to the street side of the building and is now a separate business from the hotel next door.

Opposite the Atlantic is the other St. Austell pub, **The Bishop and Wolf,** named after the two lighthouses. This was a shop until the fifties. Being an island, St, Marys has almost all supplies brought in by boat. On one of my visits there was a docks strike when even the beer failed to get through. I had the honour of drinking the last pint on the island so can honestly say that I once drank the island dry!

TALES FROM THE SNUG

In the first century AD there was a Greek physician called Dioscorides who was fairly unimpressed by the British and their drinking habits. He accused us of gathering in our ale houses to govern and adjudicate, and he complained that British ale was a compound of bad juices that did harm to the muscles and produced headaches. I think I know the beer he was talking about!

PANDORA INN

Restronguet Creek

Best approached by boat whilst exploring the Carrick Roads north of Falmouth.

The story goes that this pub got its name through a Captain Edwards who took his ship, the Pandora, to bring home Captain Bligh's rebellious lot, the mutineers of the Bounty. On the return trip he accidentally bumped into something and the Pandora was lost. The Captain eventually arrived back in Britain to face a court martial and to be dismissed the service for his incompetence. Captain Edwards, according to the story, took over the pub which was then known as The Ship, and renamed it Pandora after his own craft.

Over the years this story has found its way into local history, and it is repeated in all the guide books. In such a way, history is created, but it's apparently all a lot of baloney. Captain Edwards, it seems, never came to Cornwall. When he was court martialled, he remained in the navy and went on to be a respected admiral. Frankly, it's also a bit unlikely that he would name a pub after a ship which had apparently led to his ignominious departure from his chosen career. It's more likely that the pub was named after a packet ship upon which one of the old landlords had served, but that's a story which doesn't have quite the same ring of adventure.

Up until the early part of this century, the Pandora was a small, simple, waterside pub with only the very basic facilities, including a two-holer outdoor privy which disgorged into the stream and straight out into the estuary. Successive landlords and brewery ownerships have added bits to the building, until it is now a large pub which, in the tourist season, is a positive magnet for the visitors.

The best way to arrive at the Pandora is by boat, to tie up on the pontoon and walk the few yards to the front door, but this rather depends on the tide, and there is great local sport to be had in watching the yellow-welly brigade return to their dinghy after a night on the pop, to discover it high and dry on the mud.

As settings go, the Pandora is in one of the best. I find that drinking beer outdoors is a particular pleasure, it somehow tastes different. Drinking beer outdoors with a constantly changing view is just about perfect. There is always something happening on the water by the Pandora. In winter there is a rich variety of bird-life (keep an eye out for the pair of rare black swans which I am assured are to be seen there) and in summer there is a constant to-ing and fro-ing of yachts and dinghies.

Real Ales: St. Austells.

ROSELAND INN

Philleigh

Halfway between Ruan High Lanes and the King Harry Ferry, on the Roseland Peninsula.

Philleigh appears to be on the road to nowhere, but it was not always so. A medieval road once ran through here, connecting market centres along the south Cornish coast, so the village was at one time an important staging post on the coaching route to the far west of Cornwall. Pilgrims would have rested here on their way to St Michael's Mount, and in the days when most supplies were carried by water, the River Fal would have been a bustling trading centre, with much of the trade passing through Philliegh.

In the 18th century there was much unrest over the price of grain, and the government of the day felt that far too much of the stuff was being used for brewing beer, while not enough went on bread. Many families were reaching starvation point and, on the Roseland Peninsula, feelings reached a height when starving miners went on the rampage. In a near riot they rampaged through Philliegh and other local villages, looting farms and dealing not too kindly with some of the wealthier farmers and landowners.

Apart from that, nothing much has ever happened in Philliegh, although there was once a lady called Betsy Benarth who lived at Tolverne Cottage up the road, who had the misfortune to be accused of being a witch. Betsy was burnt to death at the crossroads which still bears her name, and her ghost is said to haunt the site.

Today, the Roseland is a surprisingly busy little pub, thanks to a loyal band of locals and a few visitors making their slow way through the Cornish lanes to cross the River Fal at the lovely King Harry Ferry. This has to be one of the most beautiful river crossings in the country, hidden, as it is, among the trees which grow right down to the waterside on the river banks.

The pub is the adopted home of the local rugby club which plays just down the road. Having your own rugby club is a pretty good asset for a country pub, since the players are not generally known for their abstinence, and they can be guaranteed to fill the place on otherwise quiet winter Saturdays. In summer their place is taken by the gig racing club. In recent years gig racing has shown a tremendous growth in popularity along the south coast, and more and more local communities are boasting their own gig for close-fought competitions on the water.

All in all, there's plenty to sing about at the Roseland, and they do that as well. The pub did have its own semi-official choir, but now it is confined to the occasional spontaneous sing-song when the mood is right and the beer is flowing.

REAL ALES: Bass, Marstons Pedigree, Sharps.

TALES FROM THE SNUG

Ale houses were the labour exchanges of years gone by. In the late 16th century there was a great deal of unemployment, and labourers were forced to travel far from home in the search for work. From 1531 all poor travellers were required to carry passports signed by a justice certifying their destination and reason for travel - on penalty of flogging or prison. Forged passes were obtainable at many alehouses, which were also a good source of casual work.

SEVEN STARS

Falmouth

Number One, The Moor, in the town centre on the road to the harbour.

It was Sir Walter Raleigh who first saw the potential of Falmouth. When he arrived in what was then a quiet and fairly obscure port, he rapidly realised that it was one of the finest natural harbours in the land. It also happened to be in an ideal position for guarding the Western Approaches and for launching expeditions out into the Atlantic. He got his old friend Sir Peter Killigrew to start developing the place, and Falmouth soon began to take on a new importance.

The town would certainly have had more than its fair share of ale-houses in those days, but it was in 1660, a few years after Sir Walter's death, that the Seven Stars was built. In those days the sea came right up to the door and boats would moor right outside. The area in front of the pub is now high and dry, but is still called the Moor, and you can see the old mooring rings in the pavements around the square.

There are one or two pubs in Falmouth I have yet to try, but, as far as I can see, the Seven Stars is the last of the old style pubs in the port to survive unchanged. There may be more attractive pubs on the outside, but on the inside this is hard to beat for real atmosphere, friendliness and good conversation.

It has been run by five generations of the same family since the 1870s, and the present licensee also happens to be the local vicar, the Rev. Barington-Bennett, who wisely believes that if he can reach the local community in the church, he may as well reach them in the pub as well. That doesn't mean you are liable to get a sermon with a pint, the Seven Stars is far to convivial for that.

While Falmouth has increasingly become a favourite destination for tourists, it still retains the feel of a working port. The sea remains its main reason for being there at all, and there is a nautical atmosphere about the place, particularly during the Classic Boat Festival and on the nights when the working boats of the Fal get together for racing. The shipyard, too, is enjoying new prosperity, so there is much talk in the Seven Stars of things that float.

Even the name of the pub is linked to the sea, as it comes from the seven stars by which sailors used to navigate. Contemporary sailors don't appear to have much trouble in finding these particular Seven Stars.

Real Ales: Bass, St Austell, guest ales.

SLOOP INN

St Ives

On the waterfront.

St Ives is the archetypal Cornish fishing village of the holiday brochures, with picture postcard cottages, a harbour, a sweeping bay, and a fleet of fishing boats bobbing gently at their moorings or lying lop-sidedly when the tide is out. It is best to ignore the new part of the town with its unattractive buildings creeping up the hill.

The pub belongs to the St Ives of yesterday. For centuries it was the domain of all those who earned their living, legally and illegally, from the sea. The fishing industry is now in a sorry state, and smuggling has transferred its core activities to the ferries, so The Sloop of today aims at that lucrative cash market of recent years, the tourists. Consequently the pub, dating back to the 14th century and reputed to be the oldest in St Ives, has undergone a lot of refurbishment, and at the height of the season it can get crowded, but, with its low-ceilinged bars, it still manages to retain some of the old character, particularly in the small bar.

St Ives has long been a haunt of painters, drawn to this part of Cornwall by the quality of the light. Many of these artists used The Sloop as a kind of club where they could meet and chat about their work. Being a fairly impoverished lot, their paintings and sketches often found themselves on the walls of the pub as payment for the artists' drinks. As a result, the pub has the air of a casual art gallery, with many of the works depicting local characters.

During the war, The Sloop took on the role of a kind of unofficial military headquarters when senior commandos used to meet in a back room, planning raids on enemy territory. Even the landlord was not allowed in the locked room.

As well as serving and probably brewing ale over the centuries, parts of the pub have also been used as a bake-house and a pork-house. It must have had something of a reputation, as when the laws restricting drinking on the Sabbath were relaxed, every other pub in St Ives successfully applied for a seven day licence. It took eleven attempts before such a licence was granted to The Sloop.

Real Ales: Old Speckled Hen, Courage Best, Theakstons, Ruddles.

STAR INN

St Just

At the end of the A3071 from Penzance heading west.

Just a few miles back from Lands End the wild and barren landscape hasn't changed much since the Bronze Age. For hundreds, nay thousands, of years miners have toiled long and hard here to bring tin from the ground and send supplies of it around the world. Like all miners, they probably had raging thirsts which they would take to the little town of St Just and as a result, it has something of a reputation. In 1734 the local vicar wrote that his parishioners there were "very much given to drink, especially on the Sabbath day of which they spend a great part in the ale houses." It was meant to encourage them out of their ways, but obviously had no effect as twenty years later he was still writing about their debauchery.

Things must have improved though, as in 1777 John Wesley preached in the town, attracting a huge congregation which presumably included miners.

St Just still manages to provide five watering holes within fifty yards of the main square. The Star is as Cornish as they come, with one, low-ceilinged dark walled bar, untainted by juke boxes or muzak, and beer served from the wood. When visiting feature film crews want a scene in a typical Cornish pub, they as often as not choose The Star, and many of the regular locals do look as if they have been chosen by Central Casting.

The pub boasts a collection of old bar games, including table skittles (sometimes known as devil-among-the-tailors) bar skittles, shut-the-box and shove ha'penny.

It is one of those pubs where customers provide their own entertainment. Not so long ago, live music was a common occurrence in pubs, but today it is confined to just a few. The Star is one of them, a mecca for talented 'folkies' and, on occasions, Cornish choirs. Landlord Peter Angwin is a leading light in St. Just's Choir.

As with any Cornish pub, the sea is never far away from thoughts, and in The Star a candle is kept burning as a permanent reminder of the Penlee Lifeboat Disaster.

Real Ales: St Austells.

TINNERS ARMS

Zennor

Off the B3306, halfway between Pendeen and St Ives.

Zennor is a beautiful little village nestling in a dip off the main road from St Ives to Lands End. The drive along the coast here is spectacular, with the Atlantic on one side and the remains of thousands of years of occupation on the other. After this barren landscape comes Zennor, with its sturdy cottages, water wheels, an impressive church on the hill and, of course, a good pub.

The Tinners Arms at Zennor, like so many Cornish watering holes, is surrounded by history, myths, and legends.

One story goes that many hundreds of years ago, a beautiful young mermaid used to emerge from the waters here in Pendar Cove and make her way up to Zennor church. (Quite how mermaids make their way on land I'm not sure, but don't worry about that.) This mermaid, like most mermaids, loved the sound of singing, but this one fell in love with a young chorister, one Matthew Trewhella by name.

One day after the church service, the mermaid and Matthew Trewhella just disappeared, and weren't to be seen again until some months later, when a fisherman brought his little boat into the bay. He threw his anchor overboard and was shocked to hear the sound of angry voices coming from beneath the sea. He looked over the edge of the boat into the gin clear water, and there was the beautiful mermaid and a young lad who were complaining bitterly that the anchor was blocking the way to their cave. Not surprisingly the skipper was a bit frightened about this, so he upped anchor and fled round the corner to St. Ives, where he told the story in one of the local pubs, and when he described the young lad all the locals knew exactly who it was - Matthew Trewhella.

The story of the mermaid is commemorated in the church where the oak end of one of the pews bears a carving of the girl-fish. At the Tinners Arms there's still much talk amongst the visitors of the mermaid of Zennor.

I suspect if Matthew Trewhella came back today he wouldn't notice many changes in the old place. Plain and unspoilt, with one low-beamed long bar, this is where the tin miners came to collect their pay, and no doubt where they spent much of it. At both ends of the bar are solid granite fireplaces for those long winter evenings, but in summer most people chose to drink on the secluded garden terrace.

It is such a beautiful part of Cornwall that many artists, writers and celebrities have been attracted here over the years so you never know who may be drinking next to you.

Real Ales: Sharps, Wadworths.

TALES FROM THE SNUG

The biggest revolution to affect pubs in the past thirty years has been the rapidly increasing food side of the business. Where once a drinker would be lucky to be offered a pickled egg or a sausage on a stick, it is now possible to find every conceivable type of food being served in pubs. Pub food now generates an income of over £5 billion a year, and two out of three adults regularly eat in pubs.

TRELOWARREN ARMS

Budock Water

A couple of miles west of Falmouth. Follow the signs towards Mabe and Constantine.

It was St Budoc who first got the community spirit going in Budock Water, some 1500 years ago. He was a Breton monk who arrived in Cornwall and set up a religious commune at the top of the valley. The Church of St Budock still stands on the hill above the village. Today, the community owes much of its spirit to the proprietors of the village's pub.

Some publicans take over a pub and just sit back waiting for the money to roll in. They don't last long. Other publicans realise that the pub is the centre of the community and they make an effort to bring people together by offering a good atmosphere and a variety of social events, not to mention good food and beer. They are the ones which succeed. The Trelowarren Arms is an example of the successful type, and it was justly rewarded by being one of three pubs in England to be nominated Community Pub of the Year in 1999.

Glyn and Ann took over the pub in 1992 and promptly set about refurbishing the place whilst retaining its character. Having done that, they gradually introduced a few activities which brought the community together. At the last count, the pub organised three pool teams, two cricket teams, two euchre teams, two darts teams, one football team and a Rugby team. It is also home to a twenty-eight piece brass band.

As if this wasn't enough, the pub also organises a number of events to raise money for local charities and good causes... ten thousand pounds in seven years. For a small pub it is a phenomenal achievement, and is entirely due to the enthusiasm of the licensees and the locals.

The early history of the Trelowarren Arms has been lost, but it is definitely known to have been operating as a pub since the 1840s. It is named after the Vyvyan family of Trelowarren who were the largest landowners in the area. One surviving document shows that the Rev. Sir Vyell Vyvyan leased to Redruth Brewery the public house and adjoining cottage. The agreement was for eighty years, as from March 1911, with "consideration £235.00, rent £1 0s 0d". The rent has increased a bit since then.

A decade ago there was just the one long bar. This has now been enlarged and modernised, which is just as well as custom has increased considerably since I first visited the pub. There is a dining room (no smoking) at one end, and a small back room for pool, darts, and other energetic pub pursuits.

The Trelowarren is everything a good pub should be, and if more places followed its example, the future of English Country pubs would be assured.

Real Ales: Bass.

TALES FROM THE SNUG

British real ale brewers have a fight on their hands, as lager is now the most popular beer in the country. It accounts for 32% of sales of draught beers as opposed to bitter and stout at 29.5% . (Brewers and Licensed Retailers Association, 1999)

TURKS HEAD

St Agnes

Take a helicopter or the ferry to St. Marys, and ask at the quay for the next boat to St. Agnes.

There are bad pubs, there are good pubs, and there are special pubs. To me, this one is very, very special. I just love the Turk's Head at St. Agnes. It is not the most beautiful, historic or even most interesting pub building in the land, but it does have one of the most beautiful locations. On a warm, calm summer's day there are few places to beat the little island of St Agnes, and there is something particularly pleasurable about arriving at England's most south-westerly pub by boat.

The Turk's Head overlooks the causeway between two coves and across to the island of Gugh which, incidentally, was once owned by a chap from Wimbledon who insisted that when he died he should be buried standing up amid the stones on the summit. Sadly, he forgot about the wild pigs that roamed the island, which made short shrift of the poor man's corpse.

With only a handful of permanent residents, the pub has to make the most of the daily infusion of tourists. It's run by a couple who are spoken of in reverential tones in the world of publicans. I met John and Pauline Dart when they ran the Mermaid on St. Mary's and the Lugger in Polruan. They ran great pubs then, and continue to do so at the Turks Head.

The pub was built originally as a boat house for the men of the customs and excise, and the revenue cutter was kept here. It was from here that the preventives used to go off chasing the smugglers. The building has only been a pub since 1972. Inside it is a simple long room but, if the weather is good, most customers choose to eat and drink outside to take advantage of the stunning view. If you are lucky that view may be enhanced by the island's gig-racers at practice.

So why is it called the Turk's Head? All the Scillonian islanders have got nick-names. On St. Mary's they're called 'Bulldogs', on Tresco they're 'Caterpillars', on Bryher 'Thorns', and Ginnicks on St. Martins. On St Agnes, they're called Turks because... unfortunately no one seems to know. Was it because the Turkish pirates came here in the 1500s? (the Lord Protector, Lord Godolfin was kidnapped by Turkish pirates).

The water off St Agnes is the colour and clarity of Bombay Gin and served just as icy cold, even in the middle of summer. Things can really get tough in the winter, when the Atlantic throws everything it's got at the islands, and that's a time when the tourists disappear and, for days on end, it becomes impossible to get even essential supplies to the pub. However, Pauline ensures that the freezer is always full, and the pub rarely runs dry. I can think of no better place to be stranded.

Real Ales: Burton, Fuggles Imperial, Flowers Original.

WHITE HART

Ludgvan

Two miles north east of Penzance, on the B3309.

First impressions count for a lot when entering a new pub. The experienced pub-hunter knows instantly whether or not he or she is going to enjoy a drink in these new surrounds. The White Hart looks good from the outside, with just the right amount of flowers and foliage covering the walls, a church next door, village square, (or at least, a widening of the road) in front, good pub sign, etc. Unlike so many pubs, the White Hart actually lives up to expectations the moment you go through the door. Lots of interesting dark cubby holes and corners, and a long, main room at the end of which is a welcoming bar surrounded by a generally happy band of locals.

Most people around these parts know the pub as Harry Bailey's as, for nearly forty years, Harry was the landlord here, and he has somehow left his stamp on the place. When he retired as one of Cornwall's longest serving landlords, some bright spark at the brewery (one of those who believe that all country pubs must appear as if they are still in the Dark Ages) decided to create the impression that the pub was really 'rural' and without basic facilities. All electric fittings were removed, and paraffin lamps were installed instead. Nobody was fooled. Fortunately, things have now returned to normality, and the sadly departed Harry's photograph looks down from pride of place above the bar.

The pub can be dated back to 1320, around the time that Ludgvan Church was being built. Several years later they were still scratching their heads thinking of a name, when Richard II came to the throne and, as his emblem was a white hart, it seemed like a good idea to curry favour with the king. History doesn't record if Dick was impressed, but the name has stuck.

The White Hart is used by members of several local male voice choirs who pop in for a drink and a practice. They produce a glorious sound - I reckon every pub should have a choir!

Real Ales: Bass, Marstons Pedigree.

TALES FROM THE SNUG

There must be several hundred White Hart pubs throughout the country, all named after the legendary animal. A lot of pub signs depict the animal with an ornate collar and that's because 2300 years ago, Alexander the Great is said to have captured a white stag and placed a collar of gold around its neck. Don't ask me why, but the Emperor Charlemagne did the same thing a thousand years later. When Richard II appeared at a tournament in Smithfield, London, in 1390, all his courtiers wore the emblem of the albino deer "theyre cotys, theyre armys, theyre sheldes and theyre trappours, were browdid all with whyte hertys with crones of gold about theyre necks and cheynes of gold hanging thereon." Nice!

INDEX